BEES' KNEES
BARMY ARMIES

BY
HARRY OLIVER

metro

Published by Metro, an imprint of John Blake Publishing Ltd,
3 Bramber Court, 2 Bramber Road,
London W14 9PB, England

www.blake.co.uk

First published in hardback in 2008

ISBN 978 1 84454 663 3

British Library Cataloguing-in-Publication Data:
A catalogue record for this book is available from the British Library.

Design by www.envydesign.co.uk

Printed in the UK by CPI William Clowes Beccles NR34 7TL

1 3 5 7 9 10 8 6 4 2

Papers used by John Blake Publishing are natural, recyclable products
made from wood grown in sustainable forests. The manufacturing processes
conform to the environmental regulations of the country of origin.

Every attempt has been made to contact the relevant copyright-holders,
but some were unobtainable. We would be grateful if the appropriate people
could contact us.

'Barmy Army' is a registered trademark of Barmy Army Ltd which
John Blake Publishing uses with their kind permission. This book is produced
independently of Barmy Army Ltd (the well-known cricket supporters) and is
concerned solely with the origins and history of English words and phrases.

For my wife, Joanna, the world's
finest fork chaser.

ALSO BY HARRY OLIVER

March Hares and Monkey's Uncles
The bestselling first book on
the origins of the words and
phrases we use every day.

Black Cats and April Fools
Origins of the old wives' tales and
superstitions in our daily lives.

Cat Flaps and Mousetraps
The origins of objects in our
daily lives.

Available in all good bookshops, priced £9.99.
To order a copy directly visit blake.co.uk

CONTENTS

ACKNOWLEDGEMENTS

First and foremost, a huge thanks to Steve Burdett for his invaluable research, hard work and advice. Second place goes to my wonderful wife Joanna, without whom I'd probably have taken about a hundred times longer to write this book. You are simply smashing.

Thanks to Graeme Andrew of Envy Design, who has once again put together a marvellous cover design. Mike Mosedale's illustrations are as wonderful and subtle as ever — I wouldn't want anyone else's cartoons in my books. Thanks again, Mike.

Thanks also to Clive Hebard for your editing, and for waiting for a manuscript that was late due to unforeseen circumstances.

INTRODUCTION

It seems many moons ago that I penned *March Hares and Monkeys' Uncles*, which was published in 2005 and much to my delight flew up the charts. From the sales of that book it seemed that an enormous number of people have a real interest in our language, and where our everyday phrases originate. Before I knew it I was being asked to write another book on the same subject, yet I had other ideas. I was already working on one about superstitions and old wives' tales, and was very keen to get going on another about inventions after that. The words and phrases would have to wait a while. It was a tough decision to make, but I'm glad I did.

Since 2005 I have received hundreds of emails

and letters filled with corrections and additional information about the entries in *March Hares*, as well as hundreds of suggestions for entries that might be included in another book. I have taken all of these into account, and some of them are featured in this book. As I began my research I was nervous that I might have to scrape the barrel a bit when seeking out words and phrases to write about – after all, I'd already written a book on the same subject. How wrong I was! English is endlessly rich, and it seems I'd temporarily forgotten how overwhelming a range of phrases I'd been able to choose from in the first place. There were still plenty of rich pickings to be had.

Uncovering the true origins of everyday expressions is always a challenge. Many of them have seductive myths attached to them, and it can be hard to ascertain the truth when fiction seems so much more intriguing. I have tried to get to the bottom of every entry in this book, and often the reality of a phrase's history can be a little drab when compared to the legend attached to it. Still, it is always fun to include both.

As always, I set out to inform but at the same time entertain, as nobody wants to nod off while reading about our idioms. There are thousands of phrases left to be written about, and I only wish I had the time and space to include them all. As things stand, I have tried to include the most diverting of them.

I have done my best to be as accurate as possible, but with such a vast subject there will always be errors. These aside, I am perpetually astonished and baffled by how much academic texts far more austere than this humble volume tend to disagree with one another on etymological issues. Finally, if there is anything in this book that you would like to comment on, I would love to hear from you. Drop me a line at words@blake.co.uk

Till next time, then!

Harry Oliver

CHAPTER ONE:
FOOD AND DRINK

'Why me...everytime ?'

FOOD AND DRINK

Alcohol

While most of us are familiar with the charms of alcohol, there was a time when only the fairer sex would have been well acquainted with it. The word comes from the Arabic *al kohl*, meaning a fine black powder used for eye make-up. Now time for the science: this powder was formed by sublimation (transforming a solid to a vapour) and then re-cooling back to a solid. The word entered the English language in the sixteenth century, with the definite article assumed to be part of the word, giving *alcohol*, which described any extremely fine powder. Subsequently it came to mean any fluid obtained through distillation. One such essence, alcohol of wine, and the spirit of any fermented liquor, became the best known of these and is the alcohol we know, love (and sometimes hate!) today.

Blowout

To have, or go on, a 'blowout' is to leave behind restraint and consume vast quantities of food, especially rich food of the kind you wouldn't eat every day. Certainly most of us experience the results of a blowout over the festive period. The phrase originally described a huge indulgent feast, quite crudely illustrating the swelling of the belly. In more recent times the meaning has extended to describe throwing caution to the wind and over-indulging in other things, such as alcohol.

Different Kettle of Fish

'Now that's a different kettle of fish,' we sometimes say when drawing a distinction between one matter and another. But we may be unaware that the phrase 'kettle of fish' has been around for centuries, and that when preceded by adjectives such as 'fine', 'nice' or 'pretty', the phrase was once used ironically to mean an awful mess. It seems that 'different kettle' grew out of 'fine kettle'. But why kettles, and why fish?

In the eighteenth century, long before the days of Russell and Hobbs, a kettle was any vessel used for boiling things up in, so it wasn't considered odd to fill a kettle with fish, especially if you lived near the River Tweed, close to the border between England and Scotland. Aristocrats used to hold picnics there, a practice commented upon by Thomas Newte in his *Tour of England and Scotland in 1785*: 'It is customary for the gentlemen who live near the Tweed to entertain their neighbours and friends with a Fête champêtre, which they call giving "a kettle of fish". Tents or marquees are pitched near the flowery banks of the river … a fire is kindled, and live salmon thrown into boiling kettles.' So it seems there were many fine kettles of fish to be had back then, and we can only assume that, now and again, it all went wrong – perhaps all those salmon would spill out of the kettle, maybe the kettle would boil over, or the fish tasted ghastly. In any case, such messy errors could well have led to the birth of the sardonic expression 'That's a fine kettle of fish'.

This is all very well, but it remains a bit of a mystery how our modern usage of the phrase developed. My guess is that to say 'a different kettle of fish' became a way of distinguishing between a messy thing and something less chaotic – after all, a ruined kettle of fish would have contrasted strongly with a perfect one.

Grocer

The grocer that we know today was originally a wholesaler, a *grossier*, selling the likes of tea, coffee, spices and dried fruits in bulk, or by the gross (meaning 144, from the French *gros*, big), to the vendor. The merchant who actually sold these goods to customers was known as a spicer. There is some confusion about when exactly the word 'grocer' took on its present meaning, but it may have been as early as the fourteenth century.

Hooch

A strong, illicitly distilled and distributed liquor, hooch is often also described as 'bootleg' (because bottles were hidden in boot legs) or 'moonshine' (because it was usually made at night). When the USA purchased Alaska in 1867 it made the sale of alcohol in the territory illegal. The local Tlingit Indians, living in a village called Hoochinoo, began making their own alcoholic drink. When the Alaskan gold rush started during the 1890s, the name was shortened to 'hooch', and it came to mean any poor-quality illegal alcoholic beverage.

Incidentally, 'hooch' is the only Tlingit Indian word to make it into the English language.

Ice-cream Sundae

The dish of ice cream covered in chocolate began life in America, and a charming story lies behind it. The origin of this sweet treat dates back to 1881, when chocolate sauce was used to make ice-cream sodas at Ed Berners' soda fountain in Two Rivers, Wisconsin. One day a man named George Hallauer asked him to put some of the chocolate sauce over a dish of ice cream. In a 1929 interview Berners said he'd been unsure if it was a good idea and protested. But Hallauer answered, 'I'll try anything once,' and got his way. A new concoction was born, and it soon became very popular.

Berners started experimenting with different flavours and fancy names. He credits the term 'Sunday' to another ice-cream parlour in nearby Manitowoc. Seeing the popularity of the dish in Two Rivers, owner George Giffy began selling the ice creams with toppings – but only on Sundays. Everything changed when a ten-year-old girl insisted on having a bowl of ice cream 'with that stuff on top'. It wasn't a Sunday, so George told her she couldn't have one. 'This must be Sunday,' replied the girl, 'for it is the kind of ice cream I want!' Giffy gave in and started selling the ice-cream treat every day, but called it a 'Sunday'. The origin of the odd spelling is a little obscure, but the story goes that a glass salesman, when writing up an order for the canoe-shaped bowls in which Berners served his ice-cream Sunday, misspelled 'Sunday' as 'Sundae'. Another theory is that the spelling was altered out of respect for Sunday's religious significance.

Lager
Lager is light-coloured, fizzy beer, more correctly called 'lager beer'. Literally, the word means a beer which is intended for storage, as *lager* is German for 'a store'. It has been in use in English since the 1850s.

Lollipop
The origin of the lollipop is uncertain, but one theory points to the term 'lolly' being an eighteenth-century word used in the north of England to mean 'mouth'. Accordingly, a lollipop was something that one 'popped' into the mouth. The term has been around since the mid-1700s, but originally it did not necessarily mean a hard candy mounted on a stick. The stick popped up at the turn of the twentieth century.

Tumbler

A tumbler is a short drinks glass, and all modern tumblers are designed so that they can be placed on a surface without tumbling over, which begs the question: why 'tumbler'? The answer is simple: in the seventeenth century the original glasses known as tumblers had bases that were either rounded or pointed. Naturally this made it impossible to put them down without 'tumbling' them. Some sources suggest that it was the glass-making practices of the day that prevented the glass bottoms from being flat, but this is untrue, as other perfectly functional styles of glass already existed. The truth is that the glassed were made purposely so that drinkers had to finish their drinks before setting down the glass – with obvious benefit to booze-vendors of the era.

Welsh Rabbit/Rarebit

If you order this in a restaurant expecting to have a bunny from Wales cooked to perfection and brought to your table, you will be sorely disappointed. For Welsh Rabbit, or Rarebit, has nothing to do with the twitchy-nosed little beasts – it is no more than cheese on toast with mustard. The term has been in use since the eighteenth century, and is said to have been invented as a dig at the

Welsh. Back then Wales was very poor, with most people unable to afford a nice piece of meat for their evening meal. Cheese was seen by the poor as the best meat substitute for meat. Joke against the Welsh or not, Welsh Rabbit is a tasty snack and you don't have to shoot it before you cook it.

Whole Shebang

Meaning everything, or the lot, 'the whole shebang' is a curious phrase. The problem with tracing its origin is that nobody seems to have a clue what a shebang is. Some postulate that it comes from *shebeen*, an Irish word for an unlicenced drinking den, or speakeasy. The vaguely humorous notion that the phrase was borne out of a drunken Irishman's tendency to try to take on 'the whole shebang' – i.e. everyone enjoying an illegal drink in the bar – has little to support it. Mark Twain first used the word in print in 1869, but, like other phrases that begin with 'the whole' ('box of dice', 'enchilada', 'nine yards'), it seems the object is only there to make a catchy phrase, and this only works if we divorce its literal meaning from its metaphorical one.

CHAPTER TWO:
MILITARY

MILITARY

Big Shot
Used to refer to a particularly important person, this twentieth-century phrase developed out of the previous century's 'big gun', which meant the same thing. A shot is a missile for a cannon or gun, and rather obviously a 'big shot', like an important person, is going to be more powerful than lesser weapons.

Braille
In 1829 Louis Braille, a blind French musician, refined this method of communication and arrived at the reading and writing system for the blind that we know today. Braille originates from an earlier, more primitive system which was actually designed

to facilitate night writing by Napoleon's army. The raised bumps on the paper could be interpreted in the dark without need for a light and so exposure of the soldier to enemy snipers was avoided.

Fifth Column

A fifth column is a clandestine group of subversive agents working to undermine a larger group, particularly a nation. The phrase was coined in 1936, during the Spanish Civil War (1936–9), by the Nationalist General Emilio Mola. When he was leading four army columns against Madrid he described, in a radio address, his 'fifth column' within the city, composed of sympathisers intent on overthrowing the Republicans from within. Various conflicts since then have seen the expression used again, including the Second World War and the Gulf War.

Go Off Half-cocked

When something 'goes off half-cocked' it's the unsatisfactory, or worse, result of premature action, usually taken on the spur of the moment without proper preparation. The expression is rooted in the eighteenth century and, unsurprisingly, alludes to guns. A gun at 'half-cock' is effectively in the safety position, with the hammer only cocked halfway so that it cannot be fired.

Some sources claim that the phrase derives from a hunter aiming his rifle at his prey, firing and then realising his weapon was half-cocked and that he has done nothing but make a fool of himself. But this explanation doesn't account for the 'going off' part of the expression. More likely is the idea that the guns in the eighteenth century certainly weren't as reliable as they are today, and often a half-cocked firearm would discharge by accident. This idea not only fits better but more fully explains the potentially terrible repercussions of 'going off half-cocked'.

Gung Ho

Meaning very eager, zealous or enthusiastic, a 'gung ho approach' is something we tend to consider rather bullish and unwise. The adjective derives from the Chinese *kung ho*, meaning to work together, and during the Second World War it was embraced by United States' Marines and even became the motto of 'Carlson's Raiders,' the nickname for a guerrilla unit of soldiers serving in the Pacific region under General Evans Carlson. The phrase spread throughout the Marines, and into wider American society with the release in 1943 of the war film *Gung*

Ho!, which told the story of Carlson's Raiders. It was Carlson's sometimes irresponsible and careless approach that led to the phrase being used ironically and negatively.

Hit the Ground Running

We use this upbeat phrase to signify a snappy and successful start to an event or enterprise. It's often said that the phrase originated in either the First or the Second World War. The story goes that, in order to prepare them for the realities of combat, trainee soldiers would be ordered to 'hit the ground running' when they were travelling at speed whether on a tank, boat or airplane. This may be true, but the expression existed years before either of the two world wars. By the late 1800s it was used in a literal sense in American civilian life, and the likelihood is that the Army borrowed the phrase because it so aptly describes an essential military manoeuvre. It is easy to see how the phrase came to be useful in today's fast-paced, competitive world, particularly in the business community.

Knock into a Cocked Hat

If something is 'knocked into a cocked hat', it is ruined and rendered worthless. Two possible origins have been suggested, one less convincing than the other. During the American Revolutionary War in the late eighteenth century, 'cocked hats' were worn by British and American officers. These hats, three-sided and worn with the rim turned up, were constantly going out of shape, and their uselessness was ridiculed by foot soldiers. So, to knock a fellow soldier into a cocked hat would have been to make him ineffective, to render him pointless. It's a nice story, yet while it is true that generals wore such silly hats, there is scant evidence that a phrase evolved out of this practice.

Far more plausible is the notion that the expression came from a bowling game which referred to the hats. Three-cornered Hat was a variation of ninepin bowls, in which three-corner pins were set up in a triangle. Each player had three balls per round, and if the three pins remained once the others had been knocked down, the game was all over, or 'knocked into a cocked hat'.

Stick to Your Guns

To 'stick to your guns' is to hold steady in your convictions and not be swayed by the views or actions of others. Perhaps unsurprisingly given the reference to guns, the phrase comes from military life, where the order was commonly issued to a group of soldiers to hold their ground or to an individual to stay at his post. Originally the expression was 'to stand to your guns', first recorded in the eighteenth century by Samuel Johnson's biographer James Boswell, but during the following century 'stick to your guns' came to replace it.

Use Your Loaf

This wonderful expression, an encouragement to be smart and use your head, is attached to a rather quaint myth. During the American Civil War soldiers trying to avoid enemy snipers in the forests would jab their bayonets into their daily bread ration and stick the loaf out to make it visible. If the enemy fired at the loaf, the soldiers could rest assured that they had 'used their loaf' well – by using a false 'head' they had saved their own. A diverting tale, but the truth is that the phrase is good old cockney rhyming slang. 'Loaf of bread' equals 'head'. Say no more.

CHAPTER THREE:
ANIMALS AND NATURE

ANIMALS AND NATURE

Bat out of Hell
Meaning to move extremely quickly, this phrase originally came into widespread use in Britain's Royal Flying Corps during the First World War, when a plane was said to fly 'like a bat out of hell'. The comparison with bats is easy to understand – they appear to fly very quickly indeed, and give off an air of panic. As for their being 'out of hell', you can well imagine they would wish to avoid the burning flames of hell and would fly extra-fast to get away from them. This may only be part of the explanation as to how the phrase came about, though, as it's likely that the age-old association between bats and the fearsome powers of the occult has something to do with the formulation.

Bats in Your Belfry

If you have 'bats in your belfry', you're a bit crazy. Who coined this twentieth-century phrase is a mystery, but the meaning is simple to unpack. The belfry, or bell tower, is the part of a church where the bells hang, and the tower itself sits on the body of the building. So, metaphorically, your belfry is your head. Bats are well known to hang out in belfries, and equally notorious for flying around erratically, seemingly madly. So, to have bats in your head means you've got a whole lot of odd things going on in there.

Bee in Your Bonnet

'Don't get a bee in your bonnet!' is a common adage used in conversation. Meaning 'Don't get crazy or worked up', the phrase is thought to stem from the sixteenth-century saying 'to have a head full of bees'. The metaphorical notion of a head abuzz with bees equating to craziness must have always been easy to understand, but it was the poet Robert Herrick who threw the bonnet into the mix in his 1648 'Mad Maid's Song':

> *Ah! woe is me, woe, woe is me! Alack and well-a-day!*
> *For pity, sir, find out that bee*

Which bore my love away.
I'll seek him in your bonnet brave,
I'll seek him in your eyes;
Nay, now I think they've made his grave
I' th' bed of strawberries.

To have a bee flying around the head in the perfect trap formed by a bonnet would be truly maddening. It is assumed that the alliteration of 'bee' and 'bonnet' meant that Herrick's take on the phrase stuck.

Bee's Knees

If something is 'the bee's knees', it is simply smashing, particularly good, perhaps the best. We use the phrase freely, yet the image it conjures up is a strange one. Most of us wouldn't know what a bee's knees look like, let alone why we compare wonderful things to a tiny furry body part. One theory is that the phrase puns on the word 'business', while another suggests that because bees carry pollen from flower to hive using little sacks on their legs, the wholesome goodness of what covers the bee's knee during this task is what the phrase alludes to. Unfortunately there is nothing to substantiate either claim.

What is known is that the phrase first came into use in America in the 1920s, when there was a vast explosion of animal-inspired nonsense phrases. Other examples include 'the cat's pajamas' and 'the cat's whiskers', the second of which has stood the test of time better than the first. Others fell right out of use, but it is worth listing a few examples just because they are so quirky. So, next time you're stuck for a fresh comparison, why not try 'the cat's miaow', 'the gnat's elbow', 'the monkey's eyebrows', 'the eel's ankle', 'the elephant's instep', 'the snake's hip' or the 'bullfrog's beard'.

Bête Noire
This striking phrase originated in France and is still used there and by English-speakers to describe something or someone unwanted, hated or feared. It's best to avoid a *bête noire* if possible, as it translates as 'black beast', an image that very effectively conjures up an adversary both terrifying and hard to conquer.

Birds and the Bees
This alliterative phrase rolls off the tongue when we require a euphemism for sex. For hundreds of years the phrase was used to refer to nature in general.

Then, it seems, at some point in the early twentieth century it came to mean something a little more specific, all thanks to the education system. Children needed to be told the facts of life, but in the past prudish educators did not think it proper to speak directly about the mechanics of human reproduction and so analogies were used instead. Children were told how the female bird lays eggs and how bees pollinate flowers. In this way it was hoped that they would somehow get the message about 'the birds and the bees' and not ask too many awkward questions.

Black Sheep

The 'black sheep' of a family or group of unrelated people is the one out of favour, an outsider, an oddball or a useless member. The expression originates from the eighteenth century, when the wool of a black sheep born into a herd of white sheep could not be dyed as a white sheep's could, yet it required just as much maintenance for the shepherd, making it of little worth. The colour black, particularly during the eighteenth and nineteenth centuries, was also associated with wickedness and the devil.

Bolt from the Blue

A 'bolt from the blue' is a complete surprise. The blot is a lightning bolt and the blue is the sky. Normally we expect lightning to strike only from a very dark, stormy sky, so a bolt that shoots to earth on a clear day would come as a real surprise. Although the phrase was probably around in everyday speech some years before, it was first recorded in writing in 1837. 'Arrestment, sudden as a bolt out of the blue, has hit strange victims,' wrote Scottish writer Thomas Carlyle in *The French Revolution*.

Bull in a China Shop

The image of a bull creating havoc in a china shop is a vivid one, and this phrase perfectly describes a situation where someone goes about solving a delicate problem in too rough a manner. It has not been suggested that the phrase can be traced to a real bull in a real china shop, but we can ascertain that the phrase does not date back further than the eighteenth century, for porcelain known as china was not made before then. It first appeared in print in 1834, in Frederick Marryat's novel *Jacob Faithful*. That is not to say that the British writer, who was a pal of Charles Dickens, invented the phrase. Its ultimate origin is a mystery, but one theory is that it may have been inspired by Greek writer Aesop's fable about an ass in a potter's shop. Needless to say, the animal knocks over a few fragile items.

Butterfly

We all know what a butterfly is, so wouldn't a more sensible name be 'flutterby'? After all, the little creatures appear more closely linked to fluttering than butter. It has been suggested that butterflies were originally called flutterbies, but alas that is not the case. Also posited is the theory that the name for these often beautiful winged insects goes back to medieval tales of fairies and witches disguised as butterflies that went around stealing butter when no one was looking. This too is nonsense. The word is simply an amalgamation of 'butter' and 'fly' and developed from the Old English *buterflege*. Yet the question remains: what do butterflies have to do with butter? They are not known for liking butter, and the most reasonable idea is that many species of butterfly have a creamy, butter-like colour.

Cat and Mouse

To play 'cat and mouse' with someone is to toy with them for a long time, as a cat would a mouse, with the aim of destroying them. This expression has the suffragettes (women fighting for the right to vote) in Britain at the start of the twentieth century to thank for its existence. When many of the suffragettes were arrested they would go on hunger strike – a tactic to be repeated throughout that century by other prisoners – to draw attention to their cause and embarrass the government. Various tactics were attempted by the government, including force-feeding, before it hit upon the Prisoners' Temporary Discharge for Health Act. Passed in 1913, this law allowed the prison authorities to detain a hunger-striking suffragette for so long that she became very weak and unable to actively protest. They would then release her, but she remained effectively on probation and could be arrested and forced to serve out the rest of the sentence, should she return to health and be caught breaking the law again. This law came to be known as the 'Cat and Mouse Act', and so an evocative expression was born.

Cook Your Goose

The phrase, which means to destroy someone's chances or hopes, can be traced back to a sixteenth-century event which may or may not have happened. Either way, the expression has retained currency. King Eric of Sweden had arrived to attack an enemy town. To show their contempt for the King and his small band of soldiers, the town's burghers hung a goose from a tower and then sent a message to him that asked, in effect, 'What do you want?' 'To cook your goose,' came the reply, whereupon King Eric's men set fire to the town, literally cooking the symbolic goose in the process.

Curiosity Killed the Cat

Not everyone is familiar with the 1980s pop band of the same name, but surely most people know that 'curiosity killed the cat'. In fact, this proverb is related to a sixteenth-century saying, 'Care killed the cat. A cat has nine lives, but care would wear them all out,' at which time 'care' meant sorrow or worry. This warning that worry could lead you to an early grave was the accepted version of the phrase until as recently as the early twentieth century, when 'curiosity' rather than 'care' became the downfall of the cat. Whether or not 'satisfaction brought him back', as the saying goes, remains to be seen.

Draw in Your Horns

To 'draw in (or pull in) your horns' is an idiom that describes a decision to exercise self-restraint, or draw back from a previous position, in the interests of self-preservation. It is commonly used of a pragmatic response to a change in financial circumstances. The expression, thought to date back to the fourteenth century, refers to snails' habit of retracting their horn-like eye stalks to protect them from imminent danger.

Drop like Flies

People dying or becoming ill or incapacitated one after the other in quick succession are often said to be 'dropping like flies'. The origin of the phrase is unknown, although it is easy to imagine that whoever coined it may have been thinking of the extreme brevity of the fly's life when drawing the comparison. It has been suggested that the expression is linked to the fairy tale *The Brave Little Tailor*, by the Brothers Grimm, in which a boy kills several flies with ease and makes a belt out of them, but the phrase doesn't appear in the story.

Eager Beaver

The 'eager beaver', that industrious, ambitious and often over-zealous fellow at work, can be a boon to productivity. At the same time he often has the unwelcome effect of making his colleagues look sluggish by comparison. Hence, the mildly derogatory connotations of the expression. Clearly the phrase is rooted in the widespread perception of the beaver as a tireless and enthusiastic worker, what with all that impressive dam-building, and phrases such as 'busy as a beaver' and 'beaver away' came into use in England as early as the eighteenth century. 'Eager beaver' itself was first recorded in use in the 1940s, by the army of a country that bristles with the creatures – Canada.

Grin like a Cheshire Cat

To grin like a Cheshire cat is to smile broadly and without inhibition. We can thank Lewis Carroll for the popularity of this expression. In his 1865 classic book *Alice in Wonderland*, his fictional cat is most commonly remembered for its almost complete disappearance – save for its grin. While Carroll certainly boosted the saying's currency, there are published instances of it in the work of the eighteenth-century English writer John Wolcot. Beyond this, the origins of the phrase are hard to pin down. To start with, the Cheshire cat isn't a breed of cat, but one idea is that the cats in Cheshire were grinning with satisfaction at living in a dairy-farming county famous for its cheeses as well as producing plenty of cream. Another version of the cheese theory is that in Cheshire, cheese was once sold in a mould that looked like a grinning cat. Staying with Cheshire but forgetting the cheese, another school of thought is that the paintings of grinning lions that once graced the signs of various inns throughout the county gave birth to the 'Cheshire cat'. Why grinning lions is another question.

Have a Gander

When about to take a close look at something we might say we're going to 'have a gander', a phrase that has been with us since the early twentieth century. A gander is, of course, a male goose – but just what does a goose have to do with it? Well, back in the seventeenth century 'to gander' meant to 'stretch your neck to see', as the male goose would. Now, if you were to have a gander at a gander as it waddles about, peering at everything and sticking its beak into other people's business, you'd see why we still associate the bird's name with an inquisitive look. The only difference is that we stopped using the verb 'to gander' long ago – instead we have, or take, a gander.

High Horse

Someone who gets on their 'high horse' is behaving overbearingly in a superior manner. Many an opinionated know-it-all has been told to 'get off your high horse'. The phrase dates back to the eighteenth century and alludes to army officers' practice of riding horses whose size reflected the riders' position in the military. A high-ranking officer rode a higher horse than an officer of more modest rank.

Hold Your Horses

If you're told to 'hold your horses' you're being advised to wait, hold on a moment, exercise a little patience. The phrase dates back to nineteenth-century America, first appearing as the rurally inflected 'hold your hosses'. Originally rooted in a literal instruction to a horserider to hold steady to stop the animal getting too excited, it soon became used as a more general piece of advice not to become agitated oneself. The first such recorded instance occurred in 1844, when it was employed in an attempt to placate someone on the verge of losing their temper.

In the Doghouse

Many a man reading this will know what being 'in the doghouse' is all about – any man, that is, who has endured his partner's wrath as a consequence of his actions. Forgetting a wedding anniversary or a birthday is a perfect example of such a lapse in standards. Just as a misbehaving dog is banished to the doghouse, the misbehaving man will find himself in disgrace and languishing in the metaphorical doghouse. Bad boy!

In *Peter Pan*, the children's father, Mr Darling, is particularly unpleasant to the family dog, Nana, despite her acting as a nurse to the kids. As punishment for his rotten ways, his wife sends him to live in Nana's Doghouse. J.M. Barrie wrote the book in 1904, and from that moment on the phrase 'in the doghouse' acquired a new meaning. No infallible means of getting out of the doghouse has been found, though flowers, jewellery and getting on all fours like a real dog and begging have all been attempted.

Jinx

When you feel you're in the grip of a 'jinx', or jinxed, you've succumbed to a superstitious belief that bad luck is on the cards or that a spell of some sort has been cast on you. The word is thought to come from *iunx*, the Greek word for the wryneck bird. This species was very much bound up with superstition and witchcraft simply because of the way it behaves when in the resting position, staring and twisting its neck slowly, as if very suspicious.

Keep the Wolf from the Door

To 'keep the wolf from the door' is to have enough food and money to avoid starvation and financial ruin – in short, to get by. The wolf has long been associated with a ravenous appetite – it is used in other phrases such as 'wolf (down) your food' – and as a symbol of fear and danger. The expression 'keep the wolf from the door' dates back to the fifteenth century, and various unlikely claims have been made about its origin being the tale of *The Three Little Pigs*.

Lame Duck

Used of a person who is incapacitated or ineffectual, the phrase 'lame duck' alludes to a duck being unable to keep up with the rest of the flock through lameness. It first occurred in the eighteenth century at the London Stock Exchange, where it was used to describe brokers who could not afford to pay their debts. In an industry where animal terminology features often – bulls and bears, for example – the duck is in stark contrast to these aggressive beasts.

Today the expression has come to be used widely of a person in office who is destined to be replaced but remains in the role for the time being. Usually they stay either because, as in the case of American Presidents in their second term, they are unable to be re-elected, or because they choose not to be. Tony Blair, for example, could have been seen as a 'lame duck' British prime minister once he announced that he wouldn't fight another election and Gordon Brown was waiting in the wings to succeed him.

Lead by the Nose

To 'lead by the nose' is to have control over someone – to have them do exactly what you want. The phrase derives from the practice of leading cart-drawing animals such as horses, donkeys and mules, whose nose would have a ring pierced through it so that a rope could be attached with which to control them. Cart animals have been led by the nose for millennia, but figurative reference to it dates back to the sixteenth century.

Lion's Share

This phrase, meaning the largest or most desirable portion of something, owes its origin to one of Aesop's fables. A lion and three of his friends – a fox, an ass and a wolf – go hunting. After they make a kill the lion says that he is going to keep three-quarters of the meat for himself. The reasons he provides for keeping the 'lion's share' are as follows: one quarter is for him, one quarter for his lioness and cubs, and the other quarter is for his courage. The lion then goes on to inform his friends that he is prepared to part with the remaining quarter provided one of them challenges him to a fight and defeats him. The three friends refuse to take him on, preferring to leave the entire kill to the King of the Beasts.

More than You Can Shake a Stick at

If I had an abundance of cash and someone were to ask me how much cash I had, then I could well reply with the curious phrase 'more than you can shake a stick at'. I've never seen anyone shake a stick at anything, let alone be faced with something that they could not shake a stick at. The phrase is certainly intriguing. Obviously, shaking a stick is not a friendly gesture, and you would probably only start waving one at somebody or something to achieve your own aims. One very plausible suggestion is that the expression comes from farming. A farmer faced with a massive herd of animals that he wants to control or count might find himself overwhelmed by the numbers and therefore his stick would be ineffectual.

Neither Hide nor Hair

If you've seen neither hide nor hair of someone or something it means you've seen nothing at all of them or it. This is certainly an American expression, and there a couple of stories related to its beginnings. It has been suggested that it derived from the habit of North American huntsman of saying, after a fruitless day's hunting, that they had seen 'neither hide nor hair' of any prey, where 'hide' means the hide of prey such as deer. The expression first appeared in the nineteenth century, and examples can be found in the work of American writer Mark Twain. However, some believe it comes from an inversion of the English expression 'hide *and* hair', which dates back to the 1500s and meant all of something.

One-horse Town

Most of us have come across a 'one-horse town' – some of us live in one – for it is quite simply a very small and sleepy town where very little happens. Almost every Western movie ever made features such a town, and the expression is indeed American in origin. This vivid image was first used there in the nineteenth century to depict a community so small that a single horse would be enough to meet its needs.

Swan Song

A 'swan song' is the final act or performance someone gives before they die, or, more often and less dramatically, before they retire, leave office (if a politician or other public figure) or break up (if a band). The expression derives from the ancient belief that swans spent their lives as mute birds, and that it was only with the onset of death that they would erupt into song for the first and only time. Now, this belief is clearly hogwash, but that didn't stop some pretty impressive names throughout the ages believing in it, and it is an idea that has been around since the Ancient Greeks. For example, Socrates explained to Plato that the swan was sacred to the god Apollo, and that its song at its death was in fact an expression of great joy that it was finally to join its master.

And the Greeks weren't alone. Even though records from as early as AD 77 show that people were aware it was false, the likes of Chaucer, Shakespeare, Byron and Tennyson have all referred to this romantic idea in their work. The actual phrase 'swan song' only came into the language in the 1830s, however, and was coined by Thomas Carlyle, after the German *Schwanengesang*.

Take the Bull by the Horns

When you decide to 'take the bull by the horns' you face up to difficulty and adversity directly, and with as much conviction as possible. The phrase as we know it today has been in use since late in the eighteenth century and, while not the trickiest metaphor to understand, there are a couple of theories as to its origin. And yes, they do involve bulls. Some believe that it derives from the practice whereby Spanish bullfighters, after weakening the bull, would toy with the bull by swirling their capes at them and grabbing their horns. Others believe it derives from the sport of bull running in England, which started in the thirteenth century in the court of King John and continued until it was outlawed six centuries later.

Two Shakes of a Lamb's Tail

If someone tells you they'll be back in 'two shakes of a lamb's tail', I wouldn't advise getting comfortable: it means they will be back very soon. The metaphor is a simple one – an excitable lamb shakes its tail back and forth very quickly. But why a lamb?, you may well ask. Well, that's a good question. It would appear that it's because of the perceived indefatigable energy of the frisky lambs, which would have been a common sight in the farm-reliant society in centuries past. In fact the phrase didn't come into being until the nineteenth century, and nowadays it's often shortened to 'two shakes'.

Some related alternatives exist, such as 'two shakes of the dice' and '*three* shakes of a lamb's tail', but they all mean the same thing and, if nothing else, provide a nice little breather when you need to buy some time for a simple task.

Until the Cows Come Home

'You can sit there and sulk until the cows come home but you *will* eat those greens!' a scolding mother might tell her reluctant child. 'Until the cows come home' describes what feels like a very long time. The saying dates back to the sixteenth century, when the cows would spend the night grazing in the fields before returning to the milking parlour in the morning; the phrase is all the more graphic because it conjures up the leisurely pace cows take over whatever they do.

CHAPTER FOUR:
SPORTS AND GAMES

'Have you seen a bull ?'

SPORTS AND GAMES

Aid and Abet

To aid and abet someone is to help and encourage them, more often than not in the context of crime and general naughty business. We all know what 'aid' means, but what about 'abet'? Well, it originated from the Norse word *beita*, meaning to bite. Biting became associated with being helpful through the sport of bear-baiting. Popular in fourteenth-century Britain, this was a pretty barbaric form of entertainment in which a hungry bear would be tied to a pole and set upon by a bunch of dogs. A fight would ensue, with the dogs biting the bear until it died, but often there were quite a number of canine casualties along the way. Naturally, the dogs often got a little bear-weary and needed some encouragement from their owners. The man who urged the dogs on was said to be 'abetting' them to carry on biting. It was all very nasty, which is why 'abet' came to mean to help someone do bad things.

Bear-baiting, like fox-hunting with hounds, is off the menu of British national pastimes by law – if you want to see dogs in action, try Crufts – but there are still plenty of dodgy geezers around ready to aid and abet other criminal enterprises.

Barmy Army

The 'Barmy Army' is the name of an organised group of English cricket fans who are dedicated to following the England team all over the world. According to their official website, their aim is simple: 'The Barmy Army has a stated goal – to make watching cricket more fun and much more popular. We use flags, banners, songs and chants to encourage the England team on the pitch.' The Army is a familiar sight in the world's cricket grounds, and although they can sometimes make a bit of a racket, their behaviour has always been noted for being a million miles away from hooliganism. It's clear why they are thought of as an army – they are 'fighting' for the cause of their team – but why 'barmy'?

The phrase originated in the late 1980s in Britain. Originally it formed part of a football chant, but was soon taken up by cricket fans. But it wasn't until the Australian media began using the term to describe the very lively, indeed die-hard, fans during a seemingly disastrous England tour of 1994 that the term was taken up by the world. The idea was that the fans were 'barmy' – slang for 'crazy' – for making such an enthusiastic noise when supporting such a hopeless team. But the band of fanatical supporters only got stronger, and printed its own T-shirts with the 'Barmy Army' logo. As the website proudly states, the T-shirts 'arrived on the third day of the Test and somehow it coincided with a famous and unexpected England victory. The Barmy Army was born and since then we have followed the team home and away with gusto, with pride and with a little bit of alcohol.'

Behind the Eight Ball
Used much more in the United States than in Britain, this phrase indicates a position of danger or peril from which there is little chance of escape. It originated in the pool halls of America, where a variation on the game of Kelly Pool was often played. In this particular version, players had to pot

the 15 balls – apart from the black 'eight ball' – in numerical rotation. To hit the 'eight ball' with the cue ball incurred a penalty, so if the 'eight ball' ended up between the cue ball and the next ball about to be hit, the player was said to be 'behind the eight ball'. To get out of such a spot, he would need to play a very difficult, perhaps impossible, shot. By the 1920s the phrase was in use outside pool halls.

Below the Belt
An action deemed to be 'below the belt' is grossly unfair, and a remark described in the same way is cruel and uncalled for. As one might guess, the expression comes from boxing. In 1867 the Marquis of Queensberry laid down a set of rules to regulate the hitherto wild sport of boxing and put an end to certain dangerous fighting techniques. He ruled that punches were not allowed 'below the belt', and over time this phrase came to be used more broadly to condemn any kind of unacceptable behaviour.

The Bigger They Are, the Harder They Fall
Bob Fitzsimmons was a British boxer who died in 1917, and is remembered for being a supreme sportsman who defied many of the expectations we have of boxers – how you're meant to look, how

you're intended to fight, what weight you're supposed to fight at, how old you should be to fight on for – and for coining the phrase 'The bigger they are, the harder they fall'. Fitzsimmons is said to have made the remark as he entered the ring in a fight against Ed Dunkhorst, one of the heaviest boxers ever to have lived. On occasion this American fighter weighed in for fights at over 400lb, earning the nickname 'the human freight car'. By contrast, Fitzsimmons had very skinny legs and a large upper body – it was said that he looked like a lightweight below the waist, and a heavyweight above it. The heavyweight champion of the world kept on punching until the age of 45, when he eventually lost to James J. Jeffries, a much bigger man. On that occasion it was our wordsmith who fell down.

Checkmate
Much like the cry of 'Bingo!' on a septuagenarian Saturday night out, 'Checkmate!' signals the moment of all-conquering victory for one chess player as he moves his piece or pieces into a position that prevents his opponent from moving his King without it being taken. The word comes from the Persian *shah mat*, which means 'the king is ambushed, defeated or thwarted'. However, it is a common

misconception that it originates from the Arabic for 'the King is dead'.

Gymnastics

One of the most enduringly popular of the Olympic sports, gymnastics traces its history back to Ancient Greece, where athletes received special training, alongside more intellectual pursuits, in a *gymnasium*. Persia, China, India and Ancient Rome also trained their soldiers in activities similar to gymnastics. The word derives from the Greek *gymnos*, meaning naked, which gives you some idea of the dress code at the time.

Have a Hunch

'It's just a hunch,' is what you might say when you have a sense, despite the absence of firm evidence, of how something will turn out. It has been said that the expression is related to a gambling superstition which held that it was good to rub a hunchback's hump before placing a bet or playing cards, but I can find nothing to support this explanation. The truth is more likely to be related to the development of the word 'hunch'. In the sixteenth century it was a verb meaning to push or shove. Incidentally, the word 'hunchback' came about a century later, when hunch was also used to mean 'raise into a hump'. Still the sense of pushing something out of shape remains. By the mid-nineteenth century the sense of pushing conveyed by 'hunch' had led to its being used to mean a hint or a tip. Someone who gives a hint or a tip about a future event does not always know that they are right, and it is this element of uncertainty which allowed the meaning of 'hunch' to extend to the way we use the word now.

Palm Off

Meaning to pass something unwanted on to another person, this expression comes from the world of card-playing. A player dealing the cards may take a sly look at a card he is about to deal to himself. If he doesn't like what he sees, he might hide it in the palm of his hand, deal himself the next card in the hope that he'll be luckier, and then 'palm off' the unwanted card to another, unwitting player.

Steeplechase

Horseracing around a course of obstacles started in the second half of the eighteenth century and was originally a chase between two church steeples. The first steeplechase took place in Ireland in 1752, when 'a certain Mr Callaghan and his friend, Mr

Edmund Blake, made a sporting wager to race cross country from Buttevant Church to the steeple of St Leger Church, a distance of roughly four and one-half miles'. Over time, steeplechases ceased to involve churches, and by the nineteenth century were taking place on purpose-made racecourses.

Under the Wire

If we get something done just in time we say we have got it just 'under the wire'. Anyone who has been a student is likely to be familiar with delivering a piece of work in this way. Coined at the start of the twentieth century, the phrase actually comes from horseracing, where a wire stretches out above the finishing line. However, since all the horses go under this wire when they finish, it's unclear why the expression means what it does. One theory is related to betting. When you put money on a horse, the option of betting 'each way' is available, which means that you will receive money if your horse comes in first or second place. Therefore a horse that comes in second has come in just 'under the wire'. It's is a nice idea, but not ultimately convincing.

A betting man would be more likely to back the idea that the expression is a variation of the earlier 'down to the wire', which comes from the same sport in the late nineteenth century. Coined to describe two horses running neck-and-neck towards the finishing line, it means to compete to the last moment. By extension, going 'under the wire' first would mean to win by a very small margin, and the expression probably spread from this idea to include the notion of narrowly achieving a deadline.

CHAPTER FIVE:
POLITICS

'We'll skip the "Naked truth" Mr. Hargreaves.'

POLITICS

Bite the Hand that Feeds You

The origin of this term describing utter ingratitude is attributed to British statesman Edmund Burke (1729–97). The noted political theorist and philosopher wrote in *Thoughts and Details on Scarcity*: 'And having looked to government for bread, on the very first scarcity they will turn and bite the hand that fed them.' His phrase became popular over time, and these days it is often heard in the adage 'Don't bite the hand that feeds you'.

Blood, Sweat and Tears

'I say to the House as I said to ministers who have joined this government, I have nothing to offer but blood, toil, tears, and sweat.' Thus spoke Sir Winston Churchill to the House of Commons on 13 May 1940. With the Second World War not going well for Britain, Prime Minister Churchill wanted to make very clear what was required of his fellow citizens if the situation was to be turned around. The phrase 'blood, sweat and tears' is often said to have been borne from Churchill's speech, but it wasn't. Perhaps unconsciously, Churchill drew the powerful words 'blood, toil, tears and sweat' from John Donne's poem of 1611, An Anatomie Of The World. Or he may have combined this notion with 'blood, sweat and tears', a phrase which predated him by at least a century and was used to describe the suffering of Christ.

CHAPTER SIX:
SARTORIAL MATTERS

'You shouldn't have dressed up mate,
it's only an informal barbie.'

SARTORIAL MATTERS

Best Bib and Tucker
To dress your smartest. This term dates from the late seventeenth century, when it originally referred to ladies' clothing. The bib was a very similar item to the children's bib of today, only it was more decorative than functional – after all, then as now, a lady didn't tend to dribble her food like a baby. The tucker was a piece of lace worn underneath the bib, and tucked into the neck of the dress. It would hang loosely and cover the neck and shoulders. It wasn't until the following century, when the phrase had become divorced from its literal meaning, that men too could be said to wear their 'best bib and tucker'.

Dressed to the Nines

When someone is dressed in their finest clothes we might say they are 'dressed to the nines'. As in some other English phrases that refer to 'nine' – for example, 'the whole nine yards', this particular number occurs for no obvious reason. There are several takes on the origin of the expression. One theory is that it comes from the Olde English form of the phrase, 'dressed to the eyne' – 'dressed to the eyes' – meaning a person is dressed elegantly from head to toe. Another possible derivation is from the eighteenth-century expression 'to the nines', which, while the 'nines' remains a mystery, we know was used to describe something of the best quality.

Dungarees

Wearing 'dungarees' is a fashion crime most people have committed at least once in their lifetime, but the original dungaree was simply a coarse blue cotton cloth, or calico, known in Hindi as *dungri*, that English traders brought back from Bombay in India. It was used to make work trousers, primarily for sailors, that covered the chest and were held up by straps over the shoulders, and over time this precursor to jeans became known as dungarees. The continuing popularity of dungarees can be ascribed to their usage by the US Navy during the Second World War; but then there's no accounting for taste.

Keep It Under Your Hat

To 'keep it under your hat' is to keep something a secret. One popular explanation of the phrase's origin is that medieval archers kept spare bow-strings under their hats, but as this didn't come into use until the nineteenth century it can be dismissed as fanciful. When we think about this saying literally, to keep something under your hat would be to hide it from others, and as recently as the nineteenth century men often did keep small possessions there. This explanation is far more plausible, and because the hat is a metaphor for the head, there is also the related suggestion that your head is where you plan to keep that secret.

Laugh in Your Sleeve

To 'laugh in your sleeve' is to secretly laugh at and deride someone. This phrase first emerged in the sixteenth century, when people wore clothes with sleeves capacious enough to conceal their faces and expressions when they discreetly lifted an arm. The French had a similar phrase, *rire sous cape*, or 'laugh in your cape'.

Strait-laced

If you're rigid, strict, prudish and you don't like being naughty, you're 'strait-laced' for sure. The term originated in the sixteenth century and referred to corsetry. Picture a person wearing a tightly-laced corset, held in and unable to bend – the image provides an eloquent figurative expression.

Too Big for Your Boots … and Your Breeches

When someone gets a little too cocky and arrogant we say that they have become 'too big for their boots (or their breeches)'. This vivid image of footwear or trousers which have ceased to fit conjures up a person who regards themselves as bigger and more commanding than they actually are, though it's clear to others that all that is expanding is their own sense of self-importance. The expression, referring variously to boots and breeches, can be traced back to nineteenth-century America.

CHAPTER SEVEN:
BUSINESS AND MONEY

'Great. We'll take it.'

BUSINESS AND MONEY

Bankrupt
A person who is at the point of insolvency is likely to be declared bankrupt, a legal ruling which entitles all of his or her creditors to his estate. Use of the word 'bankrupt' began in the mid-sixteenth century, when it was taken from the French *banqueroute*, which in turn derived from the Italian *banca rotta*, meaning a broken bench and referred to the table on which a banker performed his transactions.

Blackmail
If someone blackmails you, they threaten to do you harm by giving away your secrets unless you give them money, or sometimes other benefits, to

keep their mouth shut. When you set up a business, there may be the risk of blackmail in the form of extortion. Some criminals extort money from business owners in exchange for 'protection' – the owner is forced to pay money to prevent himself or his property being subjected to violence. In the seventeenth century farmers living in the Scottish Borders had to pay corrupt Highland chiefs such money.

The 'mail' in 'blackmail' has nothing to do with any postal system. It comes from the Scottish word *male*, meaning rent or tax. Individuals paid blackmail to gangs to make sure that they were not robbed. There are two stories relating to the 'black' part of the word. One is that the farmers often paid using black cattle, and the other is that 'blackmail' came about in contrast to 'whitemail', which was the name given to the legitimate rent paid in silver ('white') coins.

Feather Your Nest

If you 'feather your nest' you secure your own and your family's financial comfort and ease by amassing wealth, often at the same time as consolidating your professional and social standing. The expression clearly refers to birds building a nest and lining it with their own feathers to provide comfort and warmth for their eggs and subsequent chicks. Its first recorded use occurred in the mid-1500s.

Filthy Lucre

Used to mean money that is a bad influence, the phrase 'filthy lucre' has been around for a couple of centuries. 'Lucre' descends from the Latin *lucrum*, meaning gain or profit, and the word developed to imply illegal gain when Chaucer employed it in *The Canterbury Tales* in the late fourteenth century. The first example qualified by 'filthy' appeared in print in 1526 in the writings of William Tyndale. Over time the expression led to the adjective 'filthy rich'.

CHAPTER EIGHT:
FALSE FRIENDS

'We're lucky to have this lush vegetation.'

FALSE FRIENDS

Idiot

Idiots. We all know one. Some of us even are one – at least every now and then! The word originally comes from the Ancient Greek term for a private person who took no interest in public affairs. Its more modern meaning, of a mentally deficient person, from the French *idiote*, dates back to the fourteenth century, and from the end of the nineteenth century and into the twentieth century it was used in the medical profession to describe a severely mentally handicapped person. This usage eventually came to be viewed as offensive, and 'idiot' is now often used informally to describe someone behaving foolishly.

Lush

As an adjective, 'lush' means luxuriant and succulent, but as a noun it means something very different – a drunkard. There is no clear evidence that one meaning is related to the other, but some sources theorise that the second meaning may relate to the watery and juicy sense of the first, more pleasant one. Another possibility is that the term stemmed from an eighteenth-century actors' drinking club in London called the City of Lushington. There was a chairman, nicknamed the 'Lord Mayor', and four 'aldermen', who oversaw the wards of Poverty, Lunacy, Suicide and Jupiter. As its members 'were wont to turn night into day', it's possible that the second sense of 'lush' could be a contraction of the club's name. One thing is for sure: the words 'Lushington' and 'lush' were used in the nineteenth century to jokingly refer to drunkenness, and 'lush' in this sense is still heard in some quarters of society.

Philander

The verb 'philander' is used of men's behaviour towards women, and means to sleep around, to make love in a trifling manner, or at the very least to flirt heavily. The Ancient Greek noun *philandros*, from which it derives, combines the meaning 'loving' and 'man' in the sense of husband. Nowadays we understand a philanderer to be any man who's a bit too free with his loving, whether married or not.

Snob

A snob is someone who has an exaggerated respect for social status and wealth, and feels contempt towards those deemed to be inferior in these respects. A much-touted story about the origin of the word states that it is an abbreviation of the Latin *sine nobilate*, or 'without nobility'. The story goes that prospective students of the Universities of Oxford and Cambridge had to declare their ranking in society, and those not of noble birth were given the label 's.nob', which became 'snob'. The sense of someone having pretensions to being something they are not, or admiring those of superior standing was said to come out of this. This story is nonsense. The origin of the word is found not in the ivory towers of Oxbridge, but rather in the lowly workplace of the cobbler. In the late eighteenth century 'snob' meant a shoemaker or his apprentice, and by extension it came to be applied to all those of low social rank.

The modern use of the word 'snob', to describe a person who has pretensions to social standing, was brought about by nineteenth-century satirist William Makepeace Thackeray in his books *The Irish Sketch Book* and *The Book of Snobs*. Over time it has taken on the additional meaning of someone who looks down on others.

Windfall
A dose of unexpected good fortune or financial gain is often described as a 'windfall', a word that has been bandied around in English since the fifteenth century. Originally it referred generally to a spot of luck, but by the 1800s it had come to relate more specifically to money. The story goes that the word came about as a result of laws relating to the English nobility. The tenure of their estates forbade them to fell any timber because the wood was reserved for the use of the Royal Navy. However, they were entitled to help themselves to any trees blown down by the wind. High winds were therefore welcomed, as they increased the chance of a windfall. A nice story, but there is an unhappy ending, for it is nothing but a diverting myth. The truth is a little more dull – the word is German and simply means something blown in by the wind.

Nowadays it's often heard in the phrase 'windfall tax', which means a (usually) one-off levy imposed by a government on an industry or company, particularly a former utility, regarded as having made an exceptionally large profit.

CHAPTER NINE: LAW AND ORDER

LAW AND ORDER

Caught Red-handed

At one time this expression simply alluded to a person having bloody hands after committing murder or indulging in a bit of poaching. It derives from the Scottish expression 'red hand', used in the fifteenth century to describe criminals caught in the act. Sir Walter Scott's 1819 novel *Ivanhoe* is often cited as being the first book to contain the phrase: 'I did but tie one fellow, who was taken red handed and in the fact, to the horns of a wild stag.' Scott is frequently credited with having coined the term 'taken red-handed', but in truth he merely added 'ed' to 'red hand'. In any case he can be credited for popularising the phrase. His expression morphed into the modern 'caught red-handed' around the middle of the nineteenth century.

Hang, Draw and Quarter

Those of a nervous disposition may want to skip to the next entry, as what follows isn't pleasant reading. To be hung (or *hanged*, to be grammatically correct), drawn and quartered was punishment for what was considered, at the time of the practice, to be the most heinous of crimes: treason. It started in the thirteenth century and involved hanging the victim until they were almost dead, then disembowelling, or 'drawing', them before chopping off their head and cutting their body into quarters. These body parts would then be displayed throughout the city or even, in extreme cases, taken to various corners of the country as a warning against the perils of treason.

The punishment was abolished in 1870, after notable people had met this gruesome end in previous centuries, among them Guy Fawkes and the medieval Scottish patriot William Wallace, the hero of Mel Gibson's film *Braveheart*.

Hue and Cry

To raise a 'hue and cry' is to create a public clamour or drama about something. The idiom goes back to

English law in the period following the Norman conquest of 1066. At that time, when a crime was committed it was up to the victim and any witness to immediately cry out the alarm – the hue and cry. On hearing this, others would be obliged to drop whatever they were doing and do their best to apprehend the villain, to whom justice would often be summarily dispensed. The phrase derives from the Anglo-Norman phrase *hu e cri*: *hu* means an outcry and comes from the French *huer*, to shout, and *cri* means to cry out. The duty of citizens to perform the hue and cry was abolished early in the nineteenth century but the expression itself lives on in an informal, non-legalistic sense.

Real Estate

This means property, but at first 'real estate' seems a rather peculiar expression. Why 'real', and is there property that is 'unreal'? It turns out that the origins of the term have less to do with the nature of reality than with the law. In law the word 'real' is understood to relate to a thing rather than to a person, and the distinction is made between 'real property' and 'personal property'. The first of these is land, and anything attached to it; the second is most other things, such as money, clothes and other possessions. The idea is that real estate, a term in use since 1666, is immovable property which would be sold if the land it stood on were to be put up for sale. The movable stuff would be carted off by the seller. Nowadays, even though the term originated in England, most Britons think of it as American as a result of its wide use there and relative scarcity in its country of origin.

CHAPTER TEN:
ANCIENT TIMES

"Better than a poke in the eye with a sharp stick"...
well smart arse why don't you try it ?'

ANCIENT TIMES

Amethyst

An amethyst is a purple or violet precious quartz stone. The Ancient Greeks believed that wearing such a stone would prevent a wine drinker from becoming drunk. For the stone to have the desired protective effect, it had to be free of blemishes, clear and close in colour to the grape used for the wine in question. So, once a Greek reveller had got hold of a purple or violet stone, he could neck as much booze as he wanted, safe in the knowledge that he would remain as sharp as a knife. The Greek word *amethystos* translates as 'not drunk' or 'sober', *a* meaning without and *methy* meaning wine. Accordingly, those pretty stones became known as amethysts.

Beside Himself

We describe someone who is profoundly affected by a situation or event – most often with joy, rage or grief – as being 'beside himself'. The expression comes from the ancient notion that losing control of a mental faculty causes the person to be physically moved away from himself – to become 'beside himself'. Phrases such as 'out of his mind' and 'off his head' are rooted in a similar idea.

Call a Spade a Spade

Meaning to describe something as it is, to speak plainly and without euphemism, this phrase dates back to the Ancient Greeks. Menander was a dramatist, well known as a writer of Athenian New Comedy, and he is most often credited as the term's originator. His words were simple: 'I call a fig a fig, a spade a spade.' A few centuries later his compatriot Plutarch used the phrase when writing about the life of Philip of Macedon; he labelled the Macedonians 'a rude and clownish people who call a spade a spade'. The phrase first popped up in English in the sixteenth century, but there is a chance that it was the result of a mistranslation. The Greek for 'bowl' and 'spade' were similar, so the original phrase may have been 'to call a bowl a bowl'. We'll never know.

Kowtow

To act obsequiously and deferentially, in a servile manner, is encapsulated in the word *kowtow*, which has been in the English language for over two centuries. It stems from the Chinese word *koutou*, which means a knock on the head and refers to an ancient practice of touching the head on the ground to express respect and deference to an important person. These days the word is seldom used in China, but is alive and well in the West, where it is used figuratively.

Learn by Heart

The idea of learning something by heart, not head, is a slightly odd one, yet for the Ancient Greeks it made perfect sense. It arose from the Greek belief that the heart is the seat of intelligence and memory as well as emotion. Another reminder of this belief is the word 'record', which stems from a time when writing was not as commonplace as it is today and information had to be memorised. Formed from the Latin *re*, meaning again, and *cor*, meaning heart, it was used literally to mean to learn by heart. The word is found in English as far back as Chaucer.

Naked Truth

According to an ancient myth, this phrase meaning the plain and absolute truth originates in a fable: Truth and Falsehood went swimming. Falsehood stole the clothes that Truth had left on the river bank, but Truth refused to wear Falsehood's clothes and went naked. Thus a phrase was born.

Many a Slip between Cup and Lip

Often used as a warning that, between the time we plan to do something and the time we do it, things may well go wrong, this wonderful phrase began life in England in the sixteenth century, when the saying referred to 'between cup and mouth'. The first instance in writing in English occurs in Richard Tavener's 1539 book *Adagies*. 'Manye thynges fall betweene cuppe and the mouth,' he wrote, translating from the phrase penned in Latin by his contemporary the Dutch priest and scholar Erasmus.

Over time the phrase became 'cup and lip', presumably because the sound was crisper. Erasmus had pinched it from the Greeks, and the story goes that it originated in an incident between some heroes of Greek mythology. Ancaeus was the son of Poseidon and King of the island of Samos, which was famous for its wine. One day Ancaeus was tending his precious vines when one of his overworked slaves prophesied that his boss would never get to taste this batch of wine. Ancaeus paid no attention and went off on the voyage of the Argonauts. When he returned home, the grapes had been turned into wine and it was time for a taste. Ancaeus ordered his slave to bring him a cup so that he could prove his prophecy wrong. The slave did as he was told, but as he passed the wine to Ancaeus he warned, 'There's many a slip between cup and lip.' At the very moment Ancaeus raised the goblet to his mouth, a servant burst into the room to announce that a crazed boar was on the rampage around the vineyard. Ancaeus dropped the wine, ran out to try and save his vines, and was promptly killed by the boar. The prophecy had come true, and a phrase had come into being. A common variant replaces 'between' with the archaic 'twixt'.

Quintessence

The *Concise Oxford Dictionary* defines 'quintessence' as 'the most essential part of any substance ... the purest and most perfect form manifestation, or embodiment, of some quality or class'. Ancient and medieval philosophers thought all matter was composed of four elements, or 'essences': earth, air, fire and water. The Greek philosopher Pythagoras decided that there was a fifth essence – the ether of Aristotle – which he believed permeated everything and formed the heavenly bodies. Ether came to be considered the most important essence. Finding the 'quintessence' of things (from the Latin *quinta*, meaning fifth, and *essentia*, meaning essence) was from then on a serious business for philosophers. Its use in English dates from the seventeenth century.

Right Foot Foremost
This expression, meaning to do your best, has been in use since Shakespearian times, perhaps earlier. As for its origin, we must look to the Ancients. It seems that the Greeks thought it bad luck to do anything with the left foot before the right, as Brewer notes in an edition of the *Dictionary of Phrase and Fable* from the late nineteenth century: 'It was thought unlucky to enter a house or to leave one's chamber left foot foremost. [The Roman emperor] Augustus was very superstitious on this point. Pythagoras taught that it is necessary to put the shoe on the right foot first.' Of the Romans, Brewer also writes: 'In Rome a boy was stationed at the door of a mansion to caution visitors not to cross the threshold with their left foot, which would have been an ill omen.' The sense

of avoiding bad luck by using your best foot helped the phrase 'right foot foremost' come to mean what it does today. The same belief spawned the phrase 'put your best foot forward', which is heard more often nowadays than 'right foot foremost'. An allusion to the belief in good and bad feet is found in Shakespeare's *King John*, where the King says: 'Make haste; the better foot before.'

Tantalise

To 'tantalise' is to torture or tease someone with something that is desirable but just out of reach. We get the word from Tantalus, the son of the Ancient Greek deity Zeus. Tantalus had been a naughty boy and whispered some secrets of the gods to people who had no right to know them. Big mistake. Zeus decided to punish his son by sending him for all eternity to a deep, gloomy abyss called Tartarus. As if that wasn't enough, he threw in a little extra misery: Tantalus was forced to stand in water up to his chin, and above him hung branches of delicious fruit. Whenever he tried to eat and drink, both the food and the water receded to a point tantalisingly beyond his reach.

Vandal

A 'vandal' is a terrible individual who ignorantly and intentionally destroys precious and lovely things such as works of art and architectural treasures. The original 'Vandals' were a Germanic tribe who invaded large parts of Western Europe in the fourth and fifth centuries AD, and were most famous for capturing and plundering Rome in 455. Once in Rome, they didn't do as the Romans did, but went a bit nuts, ruthlessly mutilating and destroying the city's beautiful monuments.

Wrong Side of Bed

Tell someone you 'got out of the wrong side of bed' and you mean that you're in a bad mood or having a bad day. The phrase has its roots in a superstition that goes back to ancient times. Back then the 'right' side of bed was normally thought to be the opposite side from the one on which the bed was entered the night before. In Roman times it became common always to consider the right side as the correct side to get out of bed from, since it represented the side of good, the left being traditionally associated with the Devil. In these times of singledom and limited living space in cities, many of us have our beds up against one or more walls, so there is a good chance that we have to get out of the wrong side of bed every morning.

CHAPTER ELEVEN:
MIND AND BODY

'He spends so much time in the land of nod he might just as well emigrate for good.'

MIND AND BODY

Blow Hot and Cold

To 'blow hot and cold' is to be inconsistent in your outlook and opinion about someone or something. If you blow hot and cold on a friend, for example, it means you like them one minute but are not so keen the next. The expression comes from Aesop's fable about a man and a satyr (a mythical creature part man and part goat). One day the man was blowing on his hands, and when the satyr asked why, he said it was to warm them. Later, when the man blew on his hot porridge and explained that he did this to cool it, the satyr stormed off, complaining that he could not have anything to do with one who blows hot and cold out of the same mouth.

Cheek by Jowl

To be 'cheek by jowl' with someone is to be physically side by side with them. Anyone who has travelled on the London Underground during rush hour will be familiar with the feeling. It originated around the fourteenth century as 'cheek by cheek' before the second cheek became a jowl towards the end of the sixteenth century. Shakespeare provided its first recorded use, in 1595, in *A Midsummer Night's Dream*: 'I'll go with thee, cheek by jowl.'

Cool Your Heels

Ever been kept waiting for an appointment? What about for a train or bus? If so, you have been left to 'cool your heels', which means to be left to wait. The analogy is a simple one, in that when on the march our heels (feet) would be warm, whereas to remain still would leave them cool. It is believed to derive from an expression which first referred to horses – to cool the hoofs – in the seventeenth century.

Fingers Crossed

We've all crossed our fingers for good luck or in the hope of the desired outcome, for either ourselves or our friends, whether it's a matter of a lottery ticket, our exam results, or even our favourite sports team.

It's not surprising to discover the concept is rooted in religion, specifically Christianity, as people believed that making the sign of the cross with the fingers would ward off bad spirits and keep God on their side. Ideas about when the practice came into being are a little muddled, however. Some believe that it first occurred in the 1920s in America.

The custom of crossing your fingers that we more readily associate with young children is when they cross their fingers behind their backs to cover up a lie. Again, this is rooted in the religious belief that by making the sign of the cross you can escape divine retribution for the sin of the lie. Some believe this practice was in use as far back as Roman times, when Christians faced with religious persecution would lie about their faith but keep their fingers crossed to appease God. That's quite some difference over the time of origin, so perhaps it would be best to pick one period and keep your fingers crossed that it's correct!

Get Your Back Up

Have you ever been really annoyed or riled by someone or something? If so, whatever the cause, it clearly 'got your back up'. We have our feline friends to thank for the origin of this expression – when they're angry they arch their backs, making the hair there stand on end. Humans began figuratively 'getting their backs up' in the eighteenth century, although then it was more commonly said that your back was 'put up' or 'set up'.

Hand in Glove

Some readers will recognise the phrase as the title of the Smiths' first single, but 'hand in glove' has long been an expression used to denote a particularly close relationship between people. Originally coined in the seventeenth century, when the expression was 'hand *and* glove', it has come to mean something negative or perhaps Machiavellian, such as a politician working hand in glove with a dubious businessman. However, this negative connotation of the phrase is not replicated in American English.

In One Ear and Out the Other

When something goes 'in one ear and out the other', the recipient pretends to hear what has been said but won't remember or adhere to it; it's a common complaint of mothers when discussing their children. The imagery – of something passing unhindered through the head – fits clearly, and the expression is an ancient one, going all the way back to Roman times. It was believed to have been used in English as early as the fourteenth century, and it is featured in John Heywood's collection of proverbs in 1546. But perhaps its most amusing early use was to record in 1583 that a religious sermon 'goes in one eare and out at the other'. We can be quite sure it's been used in this context since!

Lie Through Your Teeth

'The world is flat!' someone might declare with apparent sincerity, but we would know them to be 'lying through their teeth' – that is, trying to convince a person of something the speaker knows not to be true. Of course the lie would usually be a little more difficult to gauge than this example, but the principle remains. The expression dates from the fourteenth century, when you would have lied *in* your teeth. In both cases the idea is that the liar grimaces to force the lie out as he is so aware of his deceit.

Make Your Hair Stand on End

If something makes our hair stand on end it has frightened or moved us greatly. The analogy is quite literal at times – our hairs do go up on end when we get goosebumps and it is a common muscle reaction.

This idea dates back to the Old Testament, Job 4: 'And when a spirit passed before me, the hair of my flesh stood up.' So it may come as some surprise to learn that the figurative expression as we know it only appeared for the first time in 1530, as part of a French phrase, and has been embraced by people, including Shakespeare, ever since.

Mesmerise

If you mesmerise someone, you have their complete attention and it is as if they were hypnotised. The word dates from the nineteenth century, and was coined in memory of Franz Mesmer, a Viennese physician who came up with the theory of animal magnetism. Mesmer was convinced the stars emitted magnetic forces that acted on humans and that all diseases were the result of blockages in the body that prevented the flow of these forces. He decided that magnets might redirect forces into the right places, and part of the treatment was to coax his patients into a trance and whisper suggestively to them while using his magnetic rod.

Mesmer's techniques seemed to work so well that King Louis XVI of France requested an investigation into his theories of magnetism and treatments. In 1784 the country's Faculty of Medicine concluded there was no such thing as magnetic fluid in the body, and that Mesmer's success in treating patients was due to the power of hypnotic suggestion. Mesmer died discredited in 1815, but by 1829 the word 'mesmerise' was in use to refer to people in a hypnotic trance, it referred directly to Mesmer's techniques and has remained in use, though often with a looser meaning, ever since.

Mouth-watering
Saliva is produced in the mouth when you desire food, and the anticipation of an enjoyable meal was captured perfectly in the sixteenth century with the expression 'mouth-watering'. By extension, it is now used to convey keen anticipation of other experiences too.

Not Turn a Hair
To 'not turn a hair' is to remain calm and unflustered when something occurs that would be expected to provoke strong, usually negative, emotion. If you were to break some terrible news to someone and they didn't get upset, you might say that they didn't turn a hair. The phrase, which has its roots in horseracing in the late nineteenth century, describes a horse that is unruffled at the finishing line,

whereas you would expect its exertions to have made it sweat and the hair of its coat messy.

Put Your Foot in it

Should you have the misfortune to 'put your foot in it', you do, or more usually say, something inappropriate, embarrassing or upsetting for someone without thinking – or even accidentally betray a secret. The expression, which dates back to the second half of the eighteenth century, appears to refer to stepping in, well, poo. We certainly shouldn't believe that it's a shortened version of the similar expression 'put your foot in your mouth' – even though a story does go that this particular phrase was coined in honour of gaffe-prone eighteenth-century Irish politician Sir Boyle Roche – as this only came into use in the early twentieth century.

Split Hairs

'Oh, stop splitting hairs!' you may have cried at a particularly pedantic friend or colleague. To 'split hairs' is to argue or qualify a piece of information at a needlessly trivial level. The expression dates from the seventeenth century, and alludes to the idea, current at the time, that hairs were so fine that to literally split one would be a pointless task.

Stab in the Back

To receive a 'stab in the back', in the figurative sense, of course, is to have someone behave perfectly amicably to your face before betraying your trust to their advantage and your detriment. It obviously comes from the idea of stabbing a trusted fellow from behind, which has been present in writing for many hundreds of years. The earliest and certainly one of the most famous examples occurs in the epic thirteenth-century German poem *The Nibelungenlied*, in which the dragon-slaying hero Siegfried is murdered by Hagen. This poem was to be referred to many times in the stabbed-in-the-back myth perpetuated by the Germans between the First and Second World Wars to explain their defeat in 1918. 'Stab in the back' is believed to have been used figuratively for the first time in 1916 by Irish playwright George Bernard Shaw.

Stick Your Neck Out

If you were going to take a chance on something and by so doing put yourself in a potentially vulnerable position, you would be 'sticking your neck out'. The expression derives from America in the early twentieth century, and it refers to the farmyard chicken with its neck laid out for the chop.

A more pleasant, though less likely, suggested origin of the phrase alludes to the tortoise, who must stick his neck out of his protective shell – exposing himself to danger in the process – to find his way.

Tail Between Your Legs

If you walk away from a situation with your 'tail between your legs' you are going off defeated and shamed. Coined in the nineteenth century, this expression owes its origin to man's best friend, the dog. When a vivacious dog, tail-wagging and full of beans, is confronted by something that scares him – a bath for example – he will slink away, his tail no longer wagging but tucked in between his hind legs. The metaphor stuck, and many a shamed person ever since has walked away with their tail between their legs.

CHAPTER TWELVE:
PLACES

'I'm your dominatrix from the "Slapstick and tickle" agency.'

PLACES

Bohemian

Today, if you're called 'Bohemian', it is because you are considered unconventional in your thinking, behaviour or dress. Unsurprisingly, the expression refers to Bohemia, now part of the Czech Republic, where, in centuries past, members of tribes travelling through the region to Western Europe were described as 'gypsies'. Back in the 1700s 'gypsy' and 'Bohemian' became synonymous as words for these nomadic, non-conformist types. It wasn't until after 1848 that the term became commonplace to describe struggling artists, writers and musicians, after William Thackeray referred to Becky Sharp, the anti-heroine of his novel *Vanity Fair*, as 'Bohemian'.

Bring Owls to Athens

To 'bring owls to Athens' is much like 'carrying coals to Newcastle', to do something wholly unnecessary and pointless. The expression derives from an Ancient Greek proverb: the owl was the symbol of Athens and in Greek mythology the city's patroness was Athena, the Goddess of Wisdom, who had an owl for a companion. The coins used in Athens from around the fifth century BC depicted Athena on one side and the owl on the other. So the owls in question were silver coins as well as birds. As this coinage was considered the most reliable and recognisable of money, and the silver was mined and the coins minted within the city itself, it came to be said that to 'bring owls to Athens' was an utterly needless endeavour.

Carry Coals to Newcastle

Like the previous entry, to 'carry coals to Newcastle' means to do something entirely unnecessary. The phrase derives from the fact that the area around Newcastle-upon-Tyne, in the north-east of England, was once the heart of the country's coal-mining industry. As it yielded plentiful supplies of coal, both for domestic use and for export around the globe, it was obvious that for an outsider to take any coal there and attempt to sell it would be an exercise in sheer futility. What may surprise some is just how far back the city's association with coal goes. Thomas Heywood recorded this link back in 1606, and 'carrying coals to Newcastle' is believed to have entered the language during the same century. As the local coal-mining industry died in the late twentieth century, so too has the expression all but disappeared from use, though other expressions for similarly pointless activities – for example, 'selling sand to the Sahara' – have replaced it.

Iron Curtain

The 'Iron Curtain' was the physical and symbolic divide between communist Eastern and capitalist Western Europe from the end of the Second World War to the end of the Cold War. Many of those who attempted to leave the communist East for the capitalist West met with a grim fate. It was Winston Churchill who brought the expression into general use, in his 1946 'Sinews of Peace' speech: 'From Stettin in the Baltic to Trieste in the Adriatic an iron curtain has descended across the Continent. Behind that line lie all the capitals of the ancient states of Central and Eastern Europe.'

'Salary is Latin for Salt money. I've decided to cut down your intake.'

WORK

Another String to Your Bow

If you have 'another string to your bow', you are able to do more than one thing. The term is often used in the workplace. If someone loses their job, they may well use this persuasive metaphor to boast that they have other options. The saying comes from the battlefield in the fifteenth century. Any sensible archer would carry a second string in case the one he was using broke, as with only one string he would be needlessly vulnerable.

Sabotage

The word 'sabotage', meaning to destroy something in a malicious or wanton way, and used particularly of disgruntled workers wrecking factory machinery, has been around for just over a century, and originated in France. The story goes that *sabots*, wooden shoes or clogs, were thrown by French factory workers into some machines with the aim of delaying production, and that the concept of *sabotage* was borne out of this, but this is a mere anecdote. Certainly the English word derives from the French *sabotage*, from *saboter*, meaning to walk noisily and clumsily, and this comes from *sabot*. The chances are that the phrase is somehow linked to the idea of walking loudly and making a fuss. During the First World War the word became popular, when an additional layer of meaning was added. Soldiers were instructed to sabotage the enemy's war efforts by attempting to destroy its machinery, bridges and transport networks.

Salary

Salarium, literally 'salt money', was the money any Roman soldier was given so that he could provide himself with salt. In the third century, when the term originated, and for many centuries afterwards, salt was a commodity far more costly than it is today. The English sense of the word – a fixed regular payment made by an employer – emerged in the early nineteenth century.

Tout

These days to 'tout' goods or services is to busily solicit customers in a pushy manner, but the word meant something else in the past. Until the 1800s, if you were touting you were acting as a lookout while a thief went a-thieving. This sense of the word came from the Middle English word *tuten*, meaning to peer. *Tuten* was itself related to an Anglo-Saxon word *totian*, meaning to stick out. The word came to be used in the world of commerce rather than crime when the label 'tout' was applied to men who literally stuck their heads out of their places of business looking for customers.

White-collar Worker

A 'white-collar worker' is anyone whose employment is non-manual labour – office workers, doctors and lawyers are all white-collar workers. Manual workers, often further classified as 'skilled' or 'unskilled', are 'blue-collar workers' – labourers, plumbers and mechanics are examples of blue-collar workers. Some suggest that 'white collar' derives from the fact that priests – who have worn a white clerical collar in Europe since medieval times – performed, as the only literate people in their society, the duties of lawyer, doctor, and scribe alongside those of the Church. In fact the truth is far more prosaic: the expression was coined in 1920s America and simply describes the standard white shirt that the office worker would wear at the time along with a jacket and tie. The term described salaried clerical workers, while the 'blue collar' referred to the colour of the overalls or work shirts – often denim – that the wage-earning worker would wear. However, as the former working classes are increasingly doing non-manual jobs, with the result that white-collar workers have come to far outweigh blue-collar workers, the term has lost some of its resonance.

CHAPTER FOURTEEN:
BIBLICAL

'Well we've got the devil on one side and the deep blue sea on the other. I think we should complain to the holiday rep.'

BIBLICAL

Beard the Lion
To 'beard the lion' is to confront and challenge a danger or threat head-on. The expression, not used as widely as it once was, has an ancient origin. It derives from a Latin proverb, based on a part of the Bible, in which David pursues a lion that has stolen a lamb, eventually catching the lion by the beard and slaying it. The phrase was used figuratively by the likes of Shakespeare in the sixteenth century, and is often expanded by the addition of 'in his den' to convey the idea of confronting the danger on its own territory.

Drop in the Ocean

A drop in the ocean is something very small and insignificant in the grand scheme of things, the metaphor being obvious enough – one drop, big ocean. The expression has biblical origins, first appearing in an English translation of the Bible in the fourteenth century as 'a drop in a bucket'. The bucket became an ocean in the nineteenth century, with Charles Dickens popularising the expression in *A Christmas Carol*.

Land of Nod

One would sincerely hope that nobody would be going off to the 'Land of Nod' – that is, to sleep – reading this entry, as this expression has its roots in a rather famous religious text: the Bible. The Land of Nod was where, in Genesis, Cain turned to after he had murdered his brother Abel. 'Nod' actually derives from the Hebrew 'to wander', but it was *Gulliver's Travels'* author Jonathan Swift who first gave the Land of Nod the meaning we associate with it today when he cunningly came up with the pun in *A Complete Collection of Genteel and Ingenious Conversation* in 1738.

Not Know from Adam

When you say, 'I don't know him from Adam', you mean you're so unfamiliar with someone that he could be anyone. Unsurprisingly, the phrase has biblical origins, and alludes to Adam, the first human to be created by God, as described in Genesis. Its first recorded use occurred in the eighteenth century, though it is undoubtedly older. In this phrase Adam stands for all men, so not to know someone from him is not to know that person from other men.

Set Your Teeth on Edge

Just imagining nails screeching down a blackboard can 'set your teeth on edge' – that is, make you feel physically uncomfortable. The phrase arose from the idea that eating something very sour causes that unpleasantly tingly feeling in the teeth and mouth. It is as old as the Bible, as this sentence from Jeremiah 31 illustrates: 'But everyone shall die for his own iniquity: every man that eateth the sour grape, his teeth shall be set on edge.'

Shakespeare's *Henry IV, Part I*, has the first recorded instance of the expression as we know it today, where the prospective cause of that nails-down-blackboard moment is 'mincing poetry'.

Sweat Blood

When someone claims to be 'sweating blood' they mean they are pushing themselves to the absolute limit at a task, to the point of real physical or mental pain, or both. Biblical in origin and found in Luke 22, the expression refers to the actions of Jesus when, after the Last Supper, he goes to the Mount of Olives: 'And being in anguish, He prayed more earnestly, and His sweat was like drops of blood falling to the ground.'

It was in or around the seventeenth century that this sweating of blood was adopted as a metaphor for our own endeavours, though, oddly enough, there is a rare medical condition, known as *hematidrosis*, that causes the body to literally sweat blood.

Take Under Your Wing

To 'take someone under your wing' is to help, protect and guide them, as an experienced person would do with a young apprentice. This idiom clearly comes from the example of the mother bird sheltering her chicks under her wing. It appears in the Bible, in Luke 13:34: 'How often I wanted to gather your children together, just as a hen gathers her brood under her wings, and you would not have it.'

Writing is on the Wall

To say 'the writing is on the wall' is to warn of impending disaster. The phrase has Old Testament origins. Daniel 5:4 tells how King Belshazzar, in the midst of a drunken feast, took sacred golden vessels out of the temple of Jerusalem and drank from them, toasting 'the gods of gold and silver, bronze, iron, wood and stone'. Just as soon as he'd committed this act of blasphemy, the fingers of a human hand appeared and proceeded to write upon the palace wall in Hebrew. Unable to read the text, Belshazzar had the prophet Daniel translate the words: 'God has numbered the days of your kingdom and brought it to an end; you have been weighed on the scales and found wanting; your kingdom is divided and given to the Medes and Persians.'

That night Belshazzar was slain, and Darius the Mede became King. It wasn't until the eighteenth century that the figurative sense of 'the writing on the wall', as we know it today, was first recorded in our language. Jonathan Swift, the political satirist and author of *Gulliver's Travels*, used it in his poem 'The Run Upon the Bankers' in 1720.

CHAPTER FIFTEEN:
NAUTICAL

'You're right Sir...it is the Flying Dutchman.'

NAUTICAL

Accost

Meaning to approach and address a person, perhaps a little boldly, the word 'accost' comes from the French *accoster*, meaning to come alongside, which in turn derives from the Latin *accostare*. It was originally used in nautical circles, and was spelled 'accoast', as if to mean 'lying along the coast of'. The modern meaning of the word developed from this – the idea of being by someone's side, of sidling up to talk to them, became synonymous with accosting them.

Between the Devil and the Deep Blue Sea

Referring to an undesirable, difficult position, this phrase originates from the world of sailing – it has nothing to do with the dark lord Satan. In traditional wooden ships, sailors had to caulk, or stop up, the seams between planks with hot tar to prevent the ship from leaking. The 'devil seam' was topmost in the hull, next to the scuppers (waterways or gutters) at the edge of the deck. It was thus the longest seam on the vessel and, as it was not flush like other hull seams, was the seam most likely to spring a leak. A sailor knocked down by a wave could find himself lying on the edge 'between the Devil and the deep blue sea'. Both positions could be fatal.

Cat Got Your Tongue?

Seldom heard today but at one time used by cruel teachers or parents to shy children, this phrase was often preceded by 'What's the matter…?' and serves to humiliate or punish. Rather aptly, the phrase originates from a particularly nasty form of punishment – the flogging of sailors by sea captains using cat o' nine tails whips in the nineteenth century. Being flogged by 'the cat' would cause a poor sailor such pain that they would be unable to speak – the cat literally would get their tongue.

Flying Dutchman

A certain portent of doom for any sailors reading this book – and any fans of the *Pirates of the Caribbean* films – the *Flying Dutchman* is, according to folklore, a ghost ship that sails the seas, doomed never to return home. Various versions of the story abound, but legend has it that the ship set sail in the seventeenth century and attempted to round the Cape of Good Hope against strong winds and storms, with the captain refusing to concede defeat, even if it took until Judgement Day to round the cape. Sailors spotting a ghostly ship passing in fog call it a 'Flying Dutchman'.

Give a Wide Berth

To 'give a wide berth' is to keep your distance and stay out of the way of someone or something. The expression dates back to the seventeenth century, when sailors referred to a 'wide berth' to mean giving another ship enough room on the sea to minimise the risk of collision. The modern, figurative use of the phrase embraces a much broader variety of situations, many rooted in emotional rather than purely practical considerations.

Hard Up

Nowadays the expression 'hard up' invariably means to be in financial difficulties, but, in the language of seafaring, to put a ship's helm 'hard up' meant to turn it away from the wind and avoid the storm. Someone who is, in today's parlance, 'hard up' turns away from the financial storm in the hope of surviving it.

Know the Ropes

Someone who 'knows the ropes' is well versed in all facets of something, usually an occupation or task. Such a person is, of course, able to show others the ropes, and once they themselves have learnt the ropes – well, you get the picture. The phrase came into use in the nineteenth century and is believed to have originally described the vast array of ropes used to control the sails on a vessel of the time. To 'know the ropes' was to understand and master the use of those ropes, though within that same century the expression gained the broader figurative meaning we know today.

Long Shot

If something you are hoping to achieve is a 'long shot', the chances of it happening are slim. That's why you'll often hear the expression used on the racecourse when the odds on an unlikely horse are 'long'. This expression comes from naval warfare of the mid-nineteenth century, when ships' cannons were rather inaccurate. Since cannon balls could travel only short distances, sea battles took place between ships at close range. Any shot fired at a ship that wasn't within the usual range of accuracy was called a 'long shot', and because such tactics tended to fail, the term came to mean something that is very unlikely.

Nail Your Colours to the Mast

To 'nail your colours to the mast' is to show fearlessly and proudly your opinions and beliefs. Any modern-day colour-nailer is happy to tell people where he stands. The phrase dates back to naval warfare of the eighteenth century. If a ship wished to surrender, it would lower its 'colours', or flags, to announce its position to the enemy. The story goes that ropes would sometimes be nailed to masts by sailors determined never to surrender, which meant that the colours could not be lowered. The phrase 'nail your colours to the mast' was picked up by civilian society as a perfect metaphor for sticking to your convictions.

Radar

Radar came about in 1941 and is an acronym based on 'ra(dio) d(etecting) a(nd) r(anging)'. A radar system does just that – it looks for aircraft, ships and other objects by sending out short radio waves that are then reflected back, allowing the equipment to ascertain the presence, direction and range of what is being sought.

Slush Fund

A 'slush fund' is money that is kept secret, or that need not be accounted for. These days the term is often used in the murky world of politics, but slush funds first existed aboard ships in the nineteenth century. Slush was waste fat from fried salt pork – standard seafarers' food at the time – that the ship's cook would keep and sell at various ports. The money made was shared between sailors to be spent on luxury items. 'Slush fund' slipped into the language of politics to refer to the money spent by politicians to bribe voters, who would then spend the money on special items. It also refers to unofficial money accumulated by leaders using shady means.

Take Down a Peg or Two

To 'take down a peg or two' is to illustrate to someone who is getting a little too pleased with themselves that they're not quite so good at something as they think. The phrase dates back to the sixteenth century, and there are a couple of theories as to what these pegs were. The most likely explanation is that they were used to raise and lower the flags on a ship, which would explain its similarity to the phrase 'take down a notch'. Another theory is that the pegs related to the amount of alcoholic drink in a barrel, and that to take the level down a peg or two was to help yourself to a good quantity from a barrel belonging to someone else.

Turn a Blind Eye

To 'turn a blind eye' to something is to pretend it is not happening and ignore it. The phrase is said to have originated from the mouth of Admiral Horatio Nelson. In the middle of the battle of Copenhagen in 1807, Nelson received orders from Admiral Sir Hyde Parker to withdraw from the Danes. The story goes that Nelson wilfully ignored the order, which was conveyed using flags, by putting the telescope to his blind eye and saying, 'I have the right to blindness sometimes... I really do not see the signal.' The battle continued and the Danes were beaten. Nobody is certain that this incident is what led to the birth of the expression, but there is a good chance that it did. In any event, other theories are very thin on the ground.

CHAPTER SIXTEEN:
SCIENCE AND
TECHNOLOGY

'There's your trouble...an unbalanced wheel.'

SCIENCE AND TECHNOLOGY

Alkali

Acid and alkali – we all remember them from science lessons at school. But where do these two words come from? Well, an alkali dissolves in water and gives off hydroxide ions, and an acid is a substance that when added to water gives off hydrogen ions, and each neutralises the other. The word 'alkali' derives from the Arabic *al qalȳ*, meaning the ashes of saltwort, and entered English in the fourteenth century. Saltwort is a plant which grows in alkaline soils and its ashes were used in the production of washing soda (sodium carbonate). Acid, on the other hand, didn't enter the language until the seventeenth century, and it comes from the French word *acide*.

Catherine Wheel

When 5 November rolls around, many are sure to be setting off Catherine Wheels – circular fireworks, attached to an upright support, that spin round and round when lit – and some might even ask, 'Why do we call them Catherine Wheels?' According to legend, St Catherine of Alexandria was a fourth-century evangelist who vociferously protested against the persecution of Christians during the rule of the Roman Emperor Maxentius. He had her arrested for her actions, but when he learned that his own wife had been converted to Christianity he had Catherine put to death on a breaking wheel. This was a large wheel upon which the victim would be tied and then clubbed violently before being left to die as it revolved. Legend has it that the wheel was broken by a bolt from above, but that Maxentius beheaded Catherine anyway, ensuring her martyrdom. The wheel was named in honour of St Catherine and she has played second fiddle to Guy Fawkes ever since.

Hermetically Sealed

When a container has been sealed and is completely airtight, we describe it as being hermetically sealed. Used by chemists, secretly sealed, airtight glass tubes are said to have been invented by the mythical Ancient Greek figure and founder of alchemy and astrology Hermes Trismegistus – an amalgamation of the Ancient Greek god Hermes and the Egyptian god Thoth. Writings attributed to Hermes Trismegistus were known as 'the Hermetica', and by the seventeenth century the word 'hermetic' was in general use to describe something as sealed.

CHAPTER SEVENTEEN:
ACROSS THE POND

'Shall we take a gander ?'

ACROSS THE POND

Big Apple

According to the Society for New York City History (SNYCH), there are several answers to the question of how 'the Big Apple' came to refer to New York City. Some commentators have traced the phrase to Depression-era sidewalk apple vendors, others to a Harlem nightclub, and yet others to a popular 1930s dance of the same name. It was in fact the music world that put the phrase into circulation. In the late 1930s any jazz musician speaking of a forthcoming appearance in 'the Big Apple' was lined up to play in Manhattan, then the most prestigious place in America to perform jazz. But even though they made the phrase popular,

New York's jazzmen didn't coin it, for it originated at the racecourse.

Racing was big business in those days – there were four major racecourses around New York, and three newspapers exclusively dedicated to the races. Racing writer John J. Fitzgerald was the man responsible for linking 'Big Apple' to New York. He wrote a column in the *New York Morning Telegraph*, and said that he first heard the phrase used by black stable boys who had followed the horses to the small quarter-mile tracks in New Orleans and all over the eastern USA and the Midwest. They were so happy to arrive in New York, where the big money was. To them the city was so huge and full of opportunity that they called it 'the Big Apple'. Fitzgerald liked the phrase so much that he adopted 'Around the Big Apple' as the title of his *Morning Telegraph* column. In 1997 the journalist's memory was honoured when a street sign reading 'Big Apple Corner' was erected in his name outside the hotel, off Broadway, where he had died in poverty back in 1963.

Brush-off

Many an amorous man, and woman is well acquainted with 'the brush-off', an American slang expression which came into common use early in the twentieth century. Meaning to be snubbed, dismissed or rejected summarily, it alludes graphically to the swift action of the hand used to remove crumbs from clothing.

Chew the Fat

To 'chew the fat', like 'shoot the breeze', is to while away the time chatting idly to friends or acquaintances. An American slang expression, believed to have been coined following the Civil War, it has a couple of potential origins. It is possible that its roots are nautical, as at one time sailors aboard ship ate tough salted pork, literally chewing the fat, while moaning incessantly about their lot to one another. Another theory is that the fat actually refers to the choice bits of gossip a ladies' sewing circle might tuck into. However, it is very likely that the expression is a variation of the earlier and more bovine 'chew the cud', which means to consider a matter for some time.

Even Stevens

'Even Stevens' means to be exactly equal, without so much as a hair's breadth between. It's an American slang expression, dating back to the nineteenth century, and is sometimes 'even Steven'. As to its origin, some claim it comes from horseracing and refers to the odds on a horse being 'even', but the only thing to be said for certain is that it came into being because of the appealing rhyme.

Get a Kick Out of

'I get no kick from champagne, mere alcohol doesn't thrill me at all, so tell me why should it be true, that I get a kick out of you...' goes the 1930s song. To 'get a kick out of' something is to get some fun and enjoyment from it. The expression is American slang and derives from the metaphorical 'kick' provided by whisky or other alcoholic spirits. 'Kick' was used exclusively in this sense from the 1840s, and it wasn't until the start of the twentieth century that people got a 'kick out of' other things – such as Ol' Blue Eyes (Frank Sinatra) performing Cole Porter's classic number.

Go Postal

After a particularly bad day at work, with tensions running high between colleagues, you may hear a wag quip, 'I could go postal right now.' The term is a slang expression, which means, as 'run amok' and 'go berserk' once did, to go into a sudden and uncontrollable frenzy – but in this case it defines rage in the workplace. The term was first coined in the American state of Florida in 1993, in an article in the *St Petersburg Times* newspaper that described it as an outburst following excessive workplace stress. In 1986 14 postal workers were shot dead and several more were injured by a clearly disgruntled fellow worker who then turned the weapon on himself. A series of similar incidents, though not quite on this scale, followed throughout the 1980s and 1990s, and the expression stuck.

Have a Yen

To 'have a yen' for something is to have a strong desire or hunger for it. The phrase dates back to America in the early twentieth century and emerged from the previous century's word *yin*, which applied specifically to a yearning for the opium so popular on both sides of the Atlantic. Opium came from China, as did the word which signified addiction to it – *yin* was borrowed from the Chinese *yan*, meaning craving.

Hell-bent

Someone who is 'hell-bent' on doing something is so recklessly determined they will do whatever it takes to achieve it – even at the risk of suffering damnation in hell. This expression can be traced back to America in 1835, where it first appeared in *Knickerbocker* magazine describing a group of native Indians as being 'hell-bent on carnage'. Another American expression which includes this phrase is 'hell-bent for leather', which describes moving at great speed. In fact the British equivalent is 'hell for leather' and 'hell-bent for leather' is most likely the result of combining this expression with 'hell-bent'.

Incidentally, 'hell for leather' is believed to have first come into prominence when the British Army was in India in the nineteenth century. Rudyard Kipling was responsible, in 1899, for the first written use of the phrase, which at that time described riding a horse very fast.

Hoodlum

Like a hooligan, a hoodlum is a young ruffian, usually a member of a gang. The word was coined in the 1870s in San Francisco, where it was used to describe gangs of violent youths who harassed Chinese labourers. There is some debate as to the exact origins, the most fanciful suggestion being that a reporter took the name of the gang's leader, Muldoon, and came up with the cunning plan of spelling it backwards, as Noodlum, to avoid reprisals by the thugs, but the newspaper's compositor misread the N as an H. The most likely – and far more prosaic – explanation, is that the word originated among the large German population living in the region at that time: *Huddellump* is a Bavarian dialect word meaning ragamuffin.

Jump the Gun

If you were to 'jump the gun' you would rush into action before the appropriate time and without adequate preparation. The expression is American in origin and very recent, dating back to the twentieth century, when it was first employed in the context of field sports. At the beginning of a race a pistol was used to let the runners know when to start, and to jump the gun was to set off before the pistol was fired. This would result in a penalty or even disqualification, just as metaphorically jumping the gun can have problematic consequences.

Pan Out

'It will be interesting to see how things pan out' is a phrase often used to express a degree of uncertainty, suspense, even hopefulness. The roots of this idiom are in the American gold-mining expression 'pan out', which referred to sieving gravel from a river through a pan and separating out any gold that might be lurking within it. This usage dates back to 1839, and it was as soon as the late 1860s in America that the phrase we use today, with its broader application, developed from it. It is easy to see the connection between waiting to see how much gold will be in your pan and waiting to see how things turn out generally.

Sixty-four-dollar Question

'How can peace be achieved in the Middle East?' 'That's the 64-dollar question!' When someone refers to the '64-dollar question' they are talking about a very difficult problem. Clearly the phrase is American, and it derives from the 1940s radio quiz *Take It Or Leave It*. Fans of today's *Who Wants To Be A Millionaire?* will be familiar with the format of the earlier show. Contestants faced a series of increasingly difficult questions, with the prize for the first answer being one dollar, and they could choose whether to stick with what they already had and go home, or to gamble on the next, more difficult, but twice as lucrative, question. Sixty-four dollars was the maximum prize and so this question would be the toughest, just as the £1-million question is in *Millionaire*.

The expression entered popular use in America, and when the radio show moved on to television networks the prize increased, so that in subsequent decades the programme became *The 64 Thousand Dollar Question*. The expression followed suit, and today inflation could even justify it being renamed *The 64 Million Dollar Question*. Oddly enough for such a specifically American idiom, it is widespread in Britain and versions of the show have appeared on British television. Even *Who Wants To Be A Millionaire?* had a £64,000 question.

Speakeasy

It is logical to assume the name for illicit drinking saloons in operation during the Prohibition era in America referred to the loose tongues of drinkers enjoying free, relaxed and raucous conversation within such establishments. It is also wrong. In the 1920s such a bar was called a 'speakeasy' because it made good sense to speak 'easy', which then meant quietly or softly, when asking a doorman for admission and while sitting inside. The idea was to avoid making any noise that would draw the unwanted attention of the police or upstanding but nosy neighbours.

Stiff Upper Lip

The ability to keep a 'stiff upper lip' is often ascribed to the British, particularly the English. The phrase describes the act of holding your emotions in check and not betraying any kind of perceived 'weakness', even when faced with great adversity – keeping the lip stiff so as to prevent it from quivering. So it will come as a surprise to many to learn that it originated in America. First coined in the early nineteenth century, the expression is now more readily associated with previous generations of Britons – Second World War and before – as the British are seen as being less reserved than they once were. As a prime example of this tendency, many point to the national outpouring of grief over HRH Princess Diana's death in 1997. Far fewer point to English footballer Gazza's tears at the World Cup seven years earlier.

Take for a Ride

Many of us can claim to have been 'taken for a ride', most likely by a dubious salesman or an elected politician, as this phrase means to be deceived or tricked. It derives from a slang expression used in Prohibition-era America. Back in the 1920s, warring gangsters such as the infamous Al Capone would threaten to take their enemies 'for a ride' under the pretext that it was to broker the peace, when in fact it was a ride from which they would never return.

Take to the Cleaners
Think of some of the messy divorces that have hit the front pages of newspapers the world over and you'll get an idea of what this expression means. To be 'taken to the cleaners' most often means to have a large portion of your money or other possessions taken away. It has also come to refer to suffering a huge defeat and is regularly used in sports.

The expression is American slang and derives from the older phrase 'cleaned out', which described someone who had gambled away all his money. The twentieth-century adaptation of the phrase keeps a similar meaning, though its use has spread beyond the world of gambling, and since the advent of dry cleaning has conjured up the image of some poor soul being thoroughly and professionally 'cleaned' of his money and goods.

Uncle Sam
With his wise old face, white hair, wispy white goatee, and outfit that reflects the colours of his country's flag, Uncle Sam has been the national

personification of the United States since the early nineteenth century. To find out why, we must turn our attention to the meat-packing industry, and one Samuel Wilson, who resided in Troy, New York State. Wilson was contracted to supply barrels of meat to the soldiers of the nation's army during the 1812 war, and all his barrels were stamped 'U.S.'. The troops joked that the initials stood for 'Uncle Sam', and over time anything marked with them came to be called Uncle Sam. A national symbol was born. In 1961 Samuel Wilson was officially recognised in congress as the 'progenitor of America's National symbol of Uncle Sam'.

CHAPTER EIGHTEEN:
WEATHER

'Look at that...blue sky and not a cloud in sight.'

WEATHER

Greased Lightning

Those of you who think *Grease* was John Travolta's finest hour – and even those who don't – will be aware that 'like greased lightning' means to move very fast indeed. The expression is, as you would expect, American in origin. As far back as the seventeenth century people had associated lightning with speed, and there are recorded uses of the term 'quick as lightning' at the time. With lightning simply not being quick enough for some – and no doubt with the American penchant for hyperbole to blame according to many British people at the time – the Americans decided to 'grease' the lightning in the early nineteenth century and the phrase was spawned.

Halcyon Days

Times of peace and prosperity are often called 'halcyon days'. The expression derives from the ancient belief that the seven days preceding and following the winter solstice would enjoy fine, calm weather. According to Greek myth, Alcyone discovered her husband Ceyx had drowned at sea and in her grief threw herself into the sea to share his fate. The gods turned the pair into birds, called halcyon birds after Alcyone, but we know them as kingfishers. When these birds came to build their nests next to the sea during the winter solstice, it was said that they had the power to control and calm the waters. Various types of kingfisher have names that refer to the mythical couple, and Shakespeare refers to 'halcyon days' in *Henry VI*.

Red Sky at Night

The adage 'Red Sky at night, shepherd's delight/Red Sky in the morning, shepherd's warning' has been around in one form or another since the fourteenth century. Its longevity is probably due to the fact that it is more than just an old wives' tale and does have some scientific validity. British weather tends to move from west to east, so a sun setting in a clear westerly sky and throwing its glow on to clouds in the east indicates that bad weather has passed over and that the coming conditions are fine. The opposite conditions – red sky in the morning – indicate that clear weather is soon to be replaced by clouds approaching from the west.

Storm in a Teacup

To make a 'storm in a teacup' is to make a big deal out of an insignificant matter – to make a problem seem far more important than it actually is. Although the first use of the expression was not recorded until the nineteenth century, various others describing a big fuss over a small matter date back as far as Roman times. The Latin phrase *excitare fluctus in simpulo* was recorded by the great orator Cicero, and it meant to 'cause waves in a wine ladle'. In the seventeenth century 'a storm in a cream bowl' was recorded in use and yet another variant is a 'storm in a wash basin'.

In other parts of the world, including America, the more alliterative 'tempest in a teacup' is widely used. It just goes to show that no matter when or where, there have always been people who make 'much ado about nothing', as Shakespeare observed towards the end of the sixteenth century.

CHAPTER NINETEEN:
ARTS AND ENTERTAINMENT

'Still too la de da, mate!'

ARTS AND ENTERTAINMENT

Anecdote

Everyone loves a good anecdote – usually a narrative of an amusing or interesting incident. The word derives from *anecdota*, the Greek for 'things unpublished'. The meaning changed a little thanks to Procopius, a Greek historian working under the Byzantine Emperor Justinian in the sixth century AD. Procopius was a serious writer, but he was also a cheeky fellow with a good ear for gossip. Alongside his official work, he also kept diaries about the secret lives of Greek courtiers, and much of the content was a bit saucy. Procopius did not want this work published, so he entitled it *Anecdota*. But the diaries were published, and because of all the scandalous stories they contained the term *anecdota* came to mean a little story, usually about someone.

Antics

Light-hearted, silly or downright eccentric behaviour is often called 'antics'. As an example we could point to John McEnroe's antics on the tennis court during his playing days. The Italians had a word *grottesco*, meaning grotesque, and they used this to describe some truly fantastical paintings – think centaurs, satyrs, exotic plants and mythical birds – which were discovered in the ancient baths of Titus in Rome in the sixteenth century. They also applied the word *antico* to the paintings, because they were ancient. Originally these two Italian words used to characterise the strange decorative art had a similar meaning. *Antico* was taken into the English language in the sixteenth century as 'antic', becoming synonymous with anything fantastic or overblown, not just the paintings described by its Italian antecedent. 'Grotesque' took a little time to catch up – it reached English via French a century or so later.

Beat the Band

This idiom, which dates from the late nineteenth century, originally meant to make a noise even louder than an orchestra, or band. Over time it came to describe something superlative, such as an outstanding achievement or a stupendous feat requiring great skill. Put simply, something 'beats the band' if it's the best in its field.

Bell the Cat

If you 'bell the cat', you are trying to complete a dangerous, difficult, perhaps impossible task, often for the benefit of others. The phrase has its beginnings in Aesop's fable *The Mice In Council*. A group of mice hold a meeting to work out how to deal with a cat that has been killing off many of their number. One wise young mouse suggests, 'I venture to propose that a small bell be procured, and attached by a ribbon round the neck of the Cat. By this means we should always know when she was about, and could easily retire while she was in the neighbourhood.' The young mouse's idea receives a warm welcome from all, until an older and wiser mouse pipes up and asks who is going to 'bell the cat'. Aesop's moral is that it is very easy to suggest difficult solutions to a problem, but no good if you are not prepared to implement them yourself.

Better than a Poke in the Eye with a Sharp Stick
This curious expression is used to convey the idea that something is actually rather good in the circumstances. Since almost anything is 'better than a poke in the eye with a sharp stick', the phrase is used somewhat ironically to point out that things could be much worse. Its origins are obscure, but it is linked to the iconic *Secret Policeman's Ball* series of theatre shows of 1976. Designed to raise money for Amnesty International, these comedy shows took place over several days and featured Monty Python, the Goodies and members of *Beyond The Fringe*. *A Poke In The Eye With A Sharp Stick* was the title of the first show at Her Majesty's Theatre in London's West End.

Bring Down the House
When a performer or performance gains rapturous, uninhibited applause and cheers from the audience, we say they have 'brought down the house'. Think of the standing ovation at the end of a great concert or play. The 'house' refers to the theatre or other auditorium having its walls and roof shake from a

show of appreciation so powerful it seems as if it might cause the whole building to collapse. Appropriately, then, there is a bit of dramatic licence in this expression, which is believed to have come into use in the eighteenth century.

Damp Squib

A 'damp squib' is a disappointment. We all know what 'damp' means, but what on earth is a 'squib'? The origins of the word are obscure, but we do know that in the early sixteenth century it was used to refer to both a short, punchy and satirical speech or written article and a small, hissing firework. It is easy to see the link between explosive, biting satire and a small firework going off. Obviously, if the firework was damp, it would likely fail and be something of a letdown to anyone expecting excitement and noise.

Down in the Dumps

If you're feeling a bit rubbish, you are 'down in the dumps'. The 'dumps' may be traced back to the Dutch word *domp*, meaning a dullness of mind, a mental haze, or to the German *dumpf*, meaning close, heavy, oppressive, gloomy. In Elizabethan times 'dump' was used to refer to slow, sad songs

171

and dances, and in Shakespeare's *The Taming of the Shrew* Petruchio finds his daughter Katerina looking sad and asks her if she is 'in your dumps'. So the phrase has been around since the sixteenth century. Chin up.

Ghost in the Machine and God from the Machine
The phrase 'ghost in the machine' describes the idea of the mind being an entity separate from but inhabiting the body. Originally used in philosophical and then literary circles, it has gradually become more prevalent in popular culture. British philosopher Gilbert Ryle coined the expression in 1949 as a withering dismissal of the idea of the mind and body being separate in his book *The Concept of Mind*.

Now, 'ghost in the machine' is not to be confused with 'god from the machine', from the Latin *deus ex machina*, which has nothing to do with philosophy, you may sigh with relief, and everything to do with the theatre and subsequently the cinema. The term means a hugely improbable plot twist to resolve a play or film that is proving tricky to complete – think of all those whodunits that bring out an unlikely and logic-defying killer at the end to really frustrate and disappoint the viewer and you're getting the picture. The 'god from the machine' originated in the Ancient Greek theatre, where an early type of mechanised crane allowed an actor playing a god to drop on to the stage and bring a satisfactory conclusion to the drama.

Ghostwriter

Politicians, celebrity columnists and even established authors at times have cause to call upon the talents of a 'ghostwriter', a writer hired to write on behalf of another individual. The origin of the word is straightforward: as a ghost is an invisible presence, so too is the ghostwriter – often uncredited and certainly kept out of the picture. Such writers were known simply as 'ghosts' until the late twentieth century, when 'writer' was more commonly added.

Ham Actor

The insulting description 'ham actor' is applied when an actor's performance is judged to be poor, particularly when their mannerisms are very over-the-top and lacking in any kind of naturalism or subtlety. Indeed, many a ham actor can steal a scene with his overcooked theatrics. The origins of this expression, which first cropped up in the late nineteenth or early twentieth century in America, cannot be said to be black and white, although the most persuasive explanation does indeed involve black and white. The term most likely came from 'hamfatter', which referred to the black-faced minstrel performers who removed the black make-up from their faces with ham fat. These performers were regarded as second-rate by their fellow thesps, and were even mocked in a song called 'The Ham Fat Man'. Among other theories is the idea that 'ham' is an allusion to amateur, because telegraphers used the word to describe a particularly poor or unskilled operator.

Hanky-panky

More recently used as an expression for a kiss and a cuddle, 'hanky-panky' first came into use in the nineteenth century to describe dishonest dealings and devious trickery. It is believed to have originated from the magicians of carnivals and fares as a variation on 'hocus pocus', as the illusionist would use a handkerchief during many of his tricks and 'panky', well, rhymes with 'hanky'. The first written use of the expression was in the first edition of *Punch* in 1841 but its sexual meaning did not come to predominate until the twentieth century.

Heebie-jeebies

If you're in a state of nervous anxiety or apprehension, you've got the heebie-jeebies. There is a long-standing myth surrounding the phrase which states that it is an anti-semitic slur that means a fear of Jews. This grew out of the misguided assertion that 'heebie' is related to 'Hebe', an insulting shortening of 'Hebrew'. When separated, 'heebie' and 'jeebie' don't mean anything, but the nonsense rhyming pair is a great example of one of a rash of similar coinages in 1920s America. In this instance the inventor was William 'Billy' De Beck (1890–1942), a celebrated comic-strip artist. The 'heebie-jeebies' debuted in one of his comic strips called 'Barney Google', along with a number of others, including 'horsefeathers', meaning total nonsense. Billy De Beck's cartoons were hugely popular and 'heebie-jeebies' caught the public imagination and quickly passed into common use.

In the Groove

When someone is functioning perfectly and with great, natural ease at some form of activity, or just feeling very good in general, we can say they are 'in the groove'. The idiom refers to the fact that when a vinyl record (or its precursor until 1938, the

175

shellac disc) is being played the stylus (or needle) has to sit 'in the groove' for it to play smoothly. When a stylus becomes worn it is likely to be too wide for the groove and produces a terrible sound. 'In the groove' was originally coined in the 1930s to describe an improvisational jazz band whose playing was outstanding because there was a powerful musical rapport between the members. Its use has since spread to many other areas, including fashion, where an advertisement might exhort you, 'If you want to be in the groove this winter, wear the latest coats from (insert your own high-end fashion label here).'

Jukebox

The Gullah language is a Creole tongue used by natives of the Sea Islands off the coast of the American states of South Carolina and Georgia. It is based on English, with strong influence from West and Central African languages originally taken across the Atlantic by slaves. In Gullah, the word 'jook' means disorderly and evil. Black American English picked up on this word in the early 1930s and the phrases 'jook house' and 'jook joint' were coined to mean a place where wild dances and parties were held; in other words, a den of iniquity where gambling, prostitution and drinking took place. The word 'jukebox' was used mainly in the deep South, and took time to become accepted in the 'white' areas of America, where 'automatic phonograph' was used until the late 1930s. The famous bandleader Glenn Miller was the first to publicly use the word 'jukebox', in an interview with *Time Magazine* towards the end of that decade.

Lick and a Promise

Most of us have been guilty of giving a task 'a lick and a promise' – that is, to give it a cursory effort in the thought that we will return to it properly at a later date. Dating back to the mid-nineteenth century, the phrase almost certainly alludes to the hasty lick clean a cat gives itself and was originally used to describe the half-hearted job a child would do when washing himself.

Magazine

The hundreds of periodical publications that line newsagents' shops are called 'magazines', and have been since the 1730s. Originally the word meant house, depot or store, and came to be applied to a repository, for by extension a magazine is a place to store ideas, articles and so on. The term is borrowed from *magasin* (French) and *magazzino* (Italian), words which in turn derive from the Arabic *makhazin*, which means storehouse. The first publication to use the word was *The Gentleman's Magazine*, in 1731. Founded by Edward Cave, this was a monthly mix of news and commentary on any subject the educated and literate public would be interested in, from commodity prices to Latin poetry. The writer Samuel Johnson found his first regular work with the magazine.

Play Second Fiddle

Some people are comfortable to 'play second fiddle', others cannot bear the idea. This expressive phrase means to have the subordinate role in something, from the performance of a single task with someone else to playing a continuing role in that person's life, while they hog the spotlight. If you've always assumed that the idiom derived from the role the supporting musician(s) played to the lead violinist in an orchestra, you're exactly right. It was coined some time in the early-or mid-nineteenth century, and has been used to describe a budding Robin in the shadow of his Batman ever since.

Play to the Gallery

If you do everything possible, in a rather obvious and show-boating manner, to please those witnessing your efforts, you can be said to be 'playing to the gallery'. Think of a footballer doing keepy-ups on the pitch mid-match or a politician grandstanding to a rapturous crowd, telling them everything they want to hear (without having to do the tricky political task of *delivering* it!). The phrase invariably has a negative implication, suggesting a degree of crassness in the person it is applied to. This connotation goes back to its theatrical roots in the seventeenth or eighteenth century, when it referred to a theatre's gallery, where cheap seats were occupied by those of the lower classes, who were seen by other members of the audience as lacking intelligence and discernment. So to 'play to the gallery' was to overtly and crudely appeal to this section of the audience rather than to the supposedly more sophisticated. Nowadays it is often said that someone is 'playing to the crowd', particularly in the context of sports.

Quiz

A charming story surrounds how this word, meaning an entertainment involving questions and answers, came about. It is said that a Dublin theatre owner named Richard Daly made a bet that he could coin a new word and it would be in general use around the city within 48 hours. The idea was that the public would come up with a meaning for the word. One evening he handed out to each member of the staff of his theatre a card on which was written the word 'quiz', and asked them to write this on walls all around Dublin. They did as requested and, lo and behold, by the following day the strange new word was on everyone's tongue. In no time at all it had become part of the language. It came to mean what it does because everybody was asking what it meant, so the word seemed perfect to describe a question-and-answer game.

A wonderful story, but there is one problem: it hasn't a shred of truth in it. The story came about in the 1830s, but 'quiz' had been in use since the 1790s. Its original meaning was 'odd and eccentric person', and nobody knows why, although it has been suggested that there may be some sort of connection with the Latin *qui es*, or 'Who are you?' If someone ever quizzes you about where the word 'quiz' comes from, the right answer would be 'I'm not sure', I'm afraid. Or you could just tell them the story.

See a Man about A Dog

'Excuse me, Mr Quail, I can't stop; I've got to see a man about a dog.' So says a character in the 1866 play *The Flying Scud or a Four-legged Fortune*, by the popular Irish playwright Dion Boucicault. Throughout this the phrase was employed as an excuse for calling conversations short or avoiding them in the first place, and audiences found it hilarious. Originally the phrase could well have been employed innocently in reference to a racing dog, but over time it came to be used in particular as a euphemism for either going to the toilet or visiting a mistress. These days it is seldom heard but when it is used the intention is to conceal one's true intentions.

Slapstick

There is a very physical sort of stage humour, where actors engage in stupid stunts that often lead to comic accidents, or try to play practical jokes that end up going farcically wrong. This sort of entertainment, called 'slapstick', gets its name from a stage prop first used in the sixteenth-century Italian improvised theatre known as the *Commedia dell'arte*. The *batacchio*, or slapstick, was two slats of wood tied together at one end, and when struck against something (usually another actor), it made a loud smacking noise. The idea was to produce a dramatic and amusing noise without causing injury to the hapless recipient of the blows.

Steal Your Thunder

If someone 'steals your thunder', they are stealing your ideas to make themselves look better or to put you at a disadvantage, or most likely both. There are many great anecdotes that seek to explain the origins of the phrase, some of which are too good to be true. But one of these is both good and true. In 1704 a literary critic and minor playwright named John Dennis was proud to have invented a novel way of creating the sound of thunder, and although the details of the method have been lost in time, what has remained is that his play for which the technique was designed was a flop. Production soon stopped, and within weeks a run of *Macbeth* had replaced it in the same theatre. On watching this, Dennis was infuriated to discover that his novel method for making thunder had been stolen, only to be used in the very next play that came along. 'Damn them!' he yelled. 'They will not let my play run, but they steal my thunder!' The disgruntled playwright's outburst was reported in the press and a phrase was born.

Upstage

If you are 'upstaged', your achievements are overshadowed by someone who does whatever you can do, but more impressively. In the mid-nineteenth century the stages of many theatres sloped upwards from the front of the stage to the back. An actor at the rear of the stage would have been standing higher, and so would have been more visible, than anybody else. Often the most important actor in a play would be placed 'upstage' in this way. Any other actor he addressed would have to look up to the speaker, and so would be upstaged.

Wear Your Heart on Your Sleeve

If you openly display your emotions for all the world to see, you 'wear your heart on your sleeve'. The expression is believed to have its beginnings in the chivalry of medieval times. It was a custom of jousting knights to wear on their arm a cloth or ribbon in the colours of the lady whom they were courting, or dating if you will. In doing so they were symbolically revealing their heart's innermost feelings. However, the first written record of the phrase occurs in Shakespeare's *Othello*, where Iago uses it to trick his master Othello into believing in his devotion.

Whole Gamut of Emotions

If you run the 'whole gamut of emotions', you experience a spectrum of feelings ranging from utter despair to ecstatic joy. Exhausting stuff. 'Gamut' is a shortened version of *gamma ut*, a medieval musical term representing all the notes in the musical scale. At that time *gamma* was the lowest note and *ut* was the next note up in the scale devised by Guido d'Arezzo. It wasn't until the seventeenth century that 'gamut' came to be used to represent a range, and 'the whole gamut of emotions' arose from this.

CHAPTER TWENTY:
RELIGION AND SUPERSTITION

'Do you have something less blue?'

RELIGION AND SUPERSTITION

Adam's Apple

The visible protrusion of cartilage in the front of a man's throat is known as 'Adam's apple'. There are two explanations for the origins of the term. Some believe it derives from the story of the Garden of Eden, in which Adam eats a piece of the forbidden apple offered to his partner Eve by the Serpent, and this lodges in his throat. The alternative – and far more prosaic – version is that the expression is simply a mistranslation of the Hebrew *tappuach ha adam*, or 'male bump'.

Baptism of Fire

If you are given an intense introduction to something – or you are 'thrown in at the deep end', to use another dramatic expression with a similar meaning – you undergo a 'baptism of fire'. The phrase refers to the Protestant Christian martyrs of the sixteenth century burned at the stake by Catholics who saw themselves as giving their victims a sort of baptism before they were judged by God. Napoleon is often credited with being the first to use the expression, in 1822, but he spoke of '*le baptême du fer*', which translates as 'baptism of iron'. These days it is applied to many situations, but crops up a lot in military circles to describe soldiers who are gaining their first experience of war.

Bless You

The custom of saying 'Bless you' or 'God bless you' when a person sneezes is partly due to superstition. Many sources claim that the expression dates back to the Great Plague, or 'Black Death', of the fourteenth century, when the fear of contagion led people to offer up these and similar sayings to heaven in the hope of warding off the disease. This theory is contradicted by records which show that expressions of this kind appeared in ancient times, and by the fact that the main symptoms of the Great Plague were buboes (large blisters on the body, usually appearing as lymph nodes), rashes and high fever, rather than sneezing.

In the ancient world it was thought that sneezing marked the visitation of a god who may have temporarily possessed the body of the sneezer or simply made his presence felt. So 'God bless you' would not have been an expression of pity or shock as it is usually interpreted to be today, but rather the statement 'God blesses you'. In Ancient Rome this initial positive interpretation of the visitation of a god was turned into a negative omen, and Romans usually said *absit omen*, 'Banish the omen', when a person sneezed, hoping to reverse any negative meaning implied by the sneeze.

Devil's Advocate

Most people have come across a 'Devil's advocate' at some point in their life – someone who argues against something or someone for the sake of argument – but where does the expression come from? Well, the Roman Catholic Church used to appoint two spokesmen to represent a candidate for sainthood. Arguing in favour of the canonisation would be the God's advocate (*advocatus dei*), while the Devil's advocate (*advocatus diaboli*) would proffer every conceivable argument against it. The practice was initiated by the Church in 1587 and abolished in 1983 by Pope John Paul II.

Honeymoon

There are several claims as to the origins of this word for a trip taken by newlyweds at the very start of their marriage. The oft-repeated explanation is that a sweet, natural potion of honey was sipped by the couple on each and every day of their marriage as an aphrodisiac. The term 'honeymoon' referred to the first 30 days, or lunar month, of the union. Cynics have suggested that 30 days is the length of time before affection between the couple begins to wane, just like the moon.

Lightning Never Strikes Twice

We use this phrase to reassure ourselves and others that an unusual or unpleasant event will never happen again under the same circumstances or to the same person. The proverb has been traced back to P.H. Myers, who first used it in his 1857 book *Prisoner of Borde*: 'They did not hit me at all. Lightning never strikes twice in the same place, nor cannon balls either, I presume.' Precisely how the phrase seeped into popular use is hard to trace, but it is very easy to demonstrate that there is no truth in the statement. The Empire State Building was struck over 60 times in one year, for instance. The saying is mere superstition.

It used to be said that looking directly at lightning could make you insane. Another old wives' tale portrays lightning more sympathetically, claiming that it was created by the Virgin Mary to warn people that Satan's thunder is on its way. Perhaps one of the strangest beliefs is that lightning strikes leave behind what are known as the 'Devil's pebbles' – stones in the shape of arrowheads that may possess magical properties and so should be saved if found.

Something Old, Something New, Something Borrowed, Something Blue

This popular rhyme, indicating four objects to be included in a bride's wedding outfit for good luck, did not become well known until the twentieth century and probably originated in Victorian times. Traditionally, 'something old' should be a handkerchief or shoes, and is thought to signify continuity and permanence in terms of the couple's friends. However, in an alternative version of the custom, this item can be an old garter given to the bride by a happily married woman so that she might enjoy an equally successful and happy union. 'Something new' symbolises a healthy and prosperous future for the couple. 'Something borrowed' is commonly an object of value lent by the bride's family, but this only brings good luck if the object is returned safely. A variation on the rhyme replaces 'something borrowed' with 'something golden' or 'something stolen'.

'Something blue' is thought to be fortunate because the colour represents faithfulness and constancy. Chaucer's *Squire's Tale* contains a reference to the wearing of blue to symbolise fidelity, for instance; and, in an Ancient Hebrew custom, brides reputedly wore a blue ribbon in their hair for the same reason. The rhyme sometimes finishes 'and a silver sixpence in her shoe', and accordingly a coin is placed in the bride's shoe. This is thought to symbolise wealth in married life, but in the oldest recorded versions of the custom, dating from the seventeenth century, the coin was intended to ward off evil spirits.

Take a Pew

If a pew is a bench in a church, why don't we call it a bench? The answer is that church pews used not to be benches. A 'pew' was a raised enclosure, rather like a pulpit. In the fourteenth century the word was originally spelled *puwe* and was borrowed from the French *puie*, which means a balcony or raised place. The root of the word is the Latin *podia*, which is the plural of *podium*. It was in the seventeenth century that the word 'pews' came to mean all the benches in a church, yet sources do not say why. Nowadays, when someone says 'take a pew', they may be inviting you to sit on a bench but are more likely to be offering you a chair.

Tie the Knot

The phrase 'tie the knot' may now be merely a figure of speech indicating a metaphorical union of a couple in marriage, but at one time it had a literal aspect. Centuries ago marriage ceremonies involved the symbolic tying together of threads from the couple's clothes, or else the binding of their thumbs and fingers. In India this practice continues today, and in Hindu weddings the bride's and groom's wrists are linked together with twine soaked in turmeric for good luck.

CHAPTER TWENTY ONE:
MEDICINE

'You've got bats alright...now we'll just have to determine what kind.'

MEDICINE

Cholesterol
In Greek, *chole* means bile and *stereos* means solid, while 'ol' is the suffix used by chemists to denote alcohol. Scientists put together these three elements to form the word 'cholesterol', a soft, solidified-fat-like substance that circulates in the bloodstream and is also found in the cells in the body. In medical language, cholesterol is a precursor to bile and hormone production.

Melancholy
Meaning sad and depressed, 'melancholy' used to mean a mental disorder in which patients were constantly low and down in the dumps. The

condition was named *malyncoly* in 1303, the word deriving from the French *mélancolie*. Ultimately the term stems from the Greek *melaina*, meaning black, and *chole*, meaning bile. Medieval medics believed melancholy resulted from an excess in the body of black bile, which was secreted from the spleen. Sufferers from melancholy also tended to be yellow, because of jaundice, a disease of the liver. So, melancholics were a pretty unhappy bunch, and it is easy to see how the word came to mean sadness in general.

Moron

Stupid people have been around a very long time, but the word 'moron' has only been knocking about since the early twentieth century. It comes from the Greek *moros*, meaning foolish and dull, and around 1912 it was picked up and used as a technical term by American psychologist and Eugenicist Henry Goddard, a member of the American Association for the Study of the Feeble-Minded. Goddard's 'morons' were adults with a mental age of 8–12 years on the Binet Scale, a system used to calculate such things. Like 'retarded' and 'feeble-minded', 'moron' was once an acceptable term used by professionals to describe certain people, but all three words eventually become obsolete in serious circles and remain only in colloquial use, as insults.

Quarantine

When people, or more often animals, arrive somewhere after being exposed to infectious or contagious disease, they are required to undergo a period of isolation known as quarantine. As early as the mid-fourteenth century, a quarantine programme was up and running in Venice. In order to protect the city's population from the Black Death, ships arriving from plague hotspots were made to anchor offshore for 40 days before being allowed to dock, as this length of time was deemed long enough for signs of the disease to develop. Scholars have theorised that Christ's 40 days in the desert may have inspired the Italians to decide on such a period of time. In either case, 'quarantine' derived from the Italian word *quaranta*, meaning 40. The word was used in Britain from the seventeenth century, but simply in reference to a period of isolation of any duration.

CHAPTER TWENTY TWO:
MISCELLANEOUS…

'It's going to be one of those days...just nod and agree with everything.'

MISCELLANEOUS...

Ambiguous
If something is ambiguous it is obscure, having double meaning, or doubtful and uncertain. The Latin preposition *ambi*, meaning about or around, originally preceded the verb *ago*, meaning to drive, to form *ambigo*, or to go about. This sense of uncertainty, of wandering, helped the word take on a more general meaning. By 1400 it had evolved into the French *ambiguité*, and the English word developed from this.

April Fool
The first of April, a day famed for japes, pranks and sky-high levels of irritation in reaction to

tomfoolery, was traditionally when the New Year was celebrated. As the date of the first day of the year according to the Julian calendar, 25 March, often fell during holy week, the celebrations were pushed back to 1 April. When France adopted the Gregorian calendar in the sixteenth century, the intention was that everyone should celebrate New Year's Day on 1 January. Of course, word travelled pretty slowly in the sixteenth century, and many people continued to celebrate New Year on 1 April. These people became known as *poissons d'avril* – April fish – and became the butt of many cruel and 'hilarious' practical jokes. The 'April Fool' was born, and in time the custom was adopted by other European countries and then others throughout the world.

Berserk

To phrase 'go berserk' – meaning to go into a frenzy or uncontrollable rage – is one most of us will have used without realising just how extreme the story behind it is. A word of Norse origin, 'berserk' was applied to a great warrior who fought with furious passion, like an out-of-control beast, perhaps foaming at the mouth. Some believe that it derives from 'bear coat' – Norsemen wore bear hides into battle – though more appealing, even if a myth, is the idea that they fought like and could even take on the form of bears. Others have suggested that 'bear' is in fact 'bare', meaning they didn't wear chain-mail shirts. Whether or not either theory is correct, Norse warriors were widely feared. References to Norse 'berserkers' abounded until the eleventh century, when the expression died out, only to appear in the English language for the first time in the nineteenth century, long after these crazed warriors were no more. The expression is used more broadly and colloquially today, but it is still also employed to describe the murderous frenzy that can occur in the heat of battle.

Between You, Me and the Lamppost

Conveying the idea of something about to be told in strict confidence, this phrase usually announces the imminent divulgence of gossip. It has been around for some 200 years and is found in Charles Dickens' novel *Nicholas Nickleby*, published in 1839. In stressing the fact that an inanimate object is the only other thing privileged to 'hear' the information, the expression is intended to show just how important it is that secrecy is maintained.

Bite the Dust

To 'bite the dust' is to die. These days a trend, a dream or a business – if it has ceased to be of use – can bite the dust just as easily as a person can. Although we most readily associate this expression with classic Western movies from the first half of the twentieth century, in fact it dates back to the Ancient Greeks, occurring in Homer's *Iliad*, which is believed to have been written in the eighth century BC. William Bryant's 1870 translation of this classic work coined the expression in English, though people had bitten the ground, and even licked the dust, thousands of years ago in the Bible.

Bone Up

Meaning to improve your knowledge of a subject, 'bone up' is a word whose precise derivation is rather tricky to establish. One theory suggests that it came from the ritual of polishing leather using bones, and a figurative connection with 'polishing up' your knowledge was supposedly established. Perhaps this is true, but it's difficult to find evidence of any symbolic connection between leather and knowledge. Another theory says that the expression derives from corset-making. If more whalebone was added to a corset, the garment became stronger, so it is easy to see how the comparison to knowledge might work. Yet again, what have corsets to do with expertise?

A third theory tells the story of the Victorian bookseller Henry George Bohn, who published the equivalent of today's study aids. The rather flimsy story relates that his texts were so popular that to 'Bohn up' became synonymous with hard revision. If so, why is there no evidence to support this, and why would Bohn have become bone? 'Bone up' certainly began life as a phrase in the mid-nineteenth century, but I'm afraid I don't know where it came from. Perhaps I need to bone up a little more.

Born with a Silver Spoon in Your Mouth

If you begin life cradled in the bosom of a rich family, you are said to have been 'born with a silver spoon in your mouth'. The reason for this is simple: for many years it was customary for godparents to give a silver spoon to their godchild at the infant's christening. Silver is a precious metal, and such a gift was something that most people could only hope to purchase by saving up for it. This necessity did not apply to the wealthy, of course. As a rich family would have possessed any number of silver spoons, the gift would have been superfluous for a child who, figuratively speaking, could have been fed from one from the day of its birth.

Break the Ice

We've all been there: a party with people you hardly know, where an unendurable silence hangs heavily over the room. Oh, for someone to 'break the ice'! An 'ice-breaker' in this sense makes an awkward and uncomfortable social situation more relaxed and pleasurable. The phrase derives from the maritime practice of breaking up the ice on the waterways so that ships and boats could travel along them in winter. In the sixteenth century it came to mean to set some form of endeavour in motion by creating a path for others to follow. Over the following couple of hundred years the expression became applied to social situations. Some commentators believe that Lord Byron was among the first to commit it to writing with this meaning in his unfinished poem *Don Juan*, published in 1819.

Burn the Candle at Both Ends

Used to describe a person who lives an extremely busy life, getting up early and staying up late, this phrase originated in France. *Brûler la chandelle par les deux bouts* was around in the 1600s, and originally referred to domestic wastefulness, in particular to married couples who spent money unnecessarily. Candles were not just handy but valued items, so to light one at both ends would be irresponsible and foolish. Over time the metaphor changed and the 'candle' came to represent both ends of the day, morning and night. To literally burn a candle at both ends would be to make it dwindle away very fast. The vivid figurative sense in which we use the expression warns, by analogy, of the danger of 'burning up' your health by not getting enough rest.

Caught with Your Pants Down

In truth nobody is sure about the origins of this phrase, which means to be taken completely by surprise, particularly in an embarrassing situation, so speculation is rife. From tales of American frontiersman laying down their muskets to answer the call of nature, only to be set upon by wily Indians, to the story of the tyrannical Roman Emperor Caracalla, who built the luxurious Spas of Caracalla, being killed by his guards when he was relieving himself, it seems that most people feel the expression has something to do not only with going to the loo but also making a mess of it. The phrase was not found in print until the 1950s, but this was due to fears about indecency. It is certainly older than this, but I can find no satisfactory history of the expression. The stories are amusing, though.

Double Entendre

'If I said you had a beautiful body would you hold it against me?' No, this hasn't turned into a book on the origins of terrible chat-up lines, but is an example of a double entendre. A 'double entendre' describes an expression that can be taken two ways – one literally and the other usually rude in a sexual sense. The double entendre allows dirty jokes to be present where you'd least expect it, such as family entertainment, as some people will only get the literal meaning – think, for example, of the classic James Bond films with Roger Moore. Unsurprisingly the phrase is French, coming from *double entente*, which means double meaning, and incorporated the French *entendre*, meaning to understand, which in turn comes from a Latin verb, to intend or to mean. We've been making double entendres since the seventeenth century.

Fiasco

Nowadays a situation referred to as a fiasco is generally a chaotic and disorganised affair. 'Fiasco' comes from the medieval French *flascon*, meaning flask or bottle, but it is not clear how this came to mean what it does today. There are suggestions that it derives from imperfections, such as bubbles left in the glass, in glassblowing techniques employed in Venice in the 1800s, or comes from the inferior glass used by the glassblower to make a common bottle for everyday use rather than something more ornamental.

For Crying out Loud

'Oh, for crying out loud, nothing but tennis on the television for two weeks!' you may hear some disgruntled soul announce during Wimbledon fortnight. A mild curse intended to show annoyance or surprise, 'For crying out loud' is what is known as a 'minced oath'. This is a type of euphemism that disguises a profanity or, in many cases, religious words, and it comes from a time when it was considered socially unacceptable to use the name of God in such a way (as it still is for many). 'For crying out loud' has been used as a minced oath to avoid saying 'for Christ's sake' since the early twentieth century. Another example is 'heck' for 'hell'.

French Leave

To 'take French leave' is to depart suddenly or unannounced without permission. It is most often used of a member or members of the armed forces, though perhaps more common nowadays is the similar term 'go AWOL'. In an example of the age-old custom whereby races impute certain characteristics to each other, the French refer to this kind of behaviour as *filer à l'anglaise* – to leave English-style!

The English expression has its roots in the eighteenth century, when, once again, England and France weren't on the best of terms, and this goes a long way towards explaining each party's negative view of its neighbours across the Channel. The phrase comes from a custom of that time whereby an individual at a party wishing to leave at short notice would have to find the host, make suitable excuses and apologies, and then bid farewell. So, to take French leave was simply to leave without fulfilling this duty, thereby causing embarrassment for the host.

Go Against the Grain

When you 'go against the grain' you are going against the received wisdom about doing something or against your natural inclinations. The phrase instantly brings to mind the grain of wood: if you plane or sand wood along the grain, the going is smooth, but if you go against the grain a right old mess can ensue. Similarly, going against the grain when shaving can bring discomfort. Shakespeare is believed to have produced the original first-written use of the expression, in *Coriolanus* in the first decade of the seventeenth century.

Go to Town

To 'go to town' means to do something with a great deal of effort and eagerness, so if the expression were used, for example, of someone's preparations for their wedding, we would assume it to mean that they were doing everything possible to ensure the success of the celebrations. The expression is a modern one, American in origin, but it has its roots further back in time, when, for country folk everywhere, 'going to town' would be a special occasion, even an adventure. Many would spend a good deal of time and effort preparing for what would invariably be an expensive trip.

Hold Water

If an argument or line of reasoning doesn't stand up to scrutiny and is shown to be unsound, we might say that it doesn't 'hold water'. The expression derives from a vessel's ability to literally hold water. Hundreds of years ago, people would test a potential container by filling it with water; if the water didn't leak out, the vessel was sound; if it leaked, the vessel was discarded as unsound. The metaphorical expression we use today came into being in the seventeenth century.

Hot Water

To be in 'hot water' is to find yourself in a spot of bother. Now people have been getting into bother since the dawn of man, though referring to it as 'hot water' only came into being in the sixteenth century. The expression is believed to refer to the manner in which people in castles at the time would ward off intruders – by pouring boiling water down on them from on high.

Kith and Kin

We use this thirteenth-century phrase, which originally meant country and kinsmen, to refer to our family, but for centuries it referred to friends too. In its early usage 'kith' meant friends and relatives – literally 'those known' – and derived from the Old English *cythth*, meaning native country. 'Kin' referred exclusively to family and developed from *cyn*, meaning family, race or kind.

Lackadaisical

Used nowadays to describe a person who is a bit of a layabout, this term dates from the 1700s and derives from the expression 'Lack a day!', which meant 'Shame on you, day' and was used by anyone who felt unfairly treated by it. At some point the meaning of the phrase changed a little, and it came to be uttered as an expletive cry when things went wrong. The words morphed into 'lackadaisy', and the 'ical' ending was tacked on soon afterwards. The meaning of laziness and inactivity of someone lackadaisical came from the idea of a person who was quick to blame factors other than himself for his bad luck and complained about it with frequent shouts of 'Lackadaisy!'

Lay an Egg

To 'lay an egg' is a sports expression used in America and means to fail at something absolutely, even humiliatingly. The egg is there because of its resemblance to 0, so, for example, a team that fails to score has 'laid an egg'. The phrase actually comes from British sport in the nineteenth century, when it was said of a player who had scored nothing that he was out for a 'duck egg'. Cricketers are now simply 'out for a duck' when they fail to score a single run, and the egg has migrated across the pond.

Maundy Thursday

Maundy Thursday, or Holy Thursday, is the Thursday before Easter in the Christian calendar which commemorates the Last Supper. The word 'Maundy' originates from the Gospel of John 13:34, where Jesus says, 'A new commandment I give unto you', and explains to the Apostles the importance of his washing of their feet. *Mandatum novum* is the Latin for 'a new commandment', and is the first part to be sung during the feet-washing ceremony. Over time *mandatum* mixed with Middle English and Old French (*mandé*) and passed through various guises in the thirteenth and fourteenth centuries to become 'Maundy'.

Paraphernalia

Used to mean personal belongings, equipment and accessories, this word harks back to the Greek *parapherna*, where *para* means beside or supplementary and *pherna* denotes dowry. The Romans adopted this Greek word to refer to objects that a woman could claim as her own should her husband pass away. These objects were 'extra' to her dower, or share of her husband's estate.

Pay the Piper

To 'pay the piper' is to face the inevitable, and usually unpleasant, consequences of your actions. The phrase appears in a proverb from the early seventeenth century, but its roots stretch back much earlier, to the thirteenth century and the legend of the Pied Piper of Hamelin. This tells of how the Pied Piper played his magical tune to free the German village of Hamelin of its plague of rats. When it came to paying him for his labours, however, the villagers reneged on the deal they had struck with the Pied Piper. So he had his revenge: he played his magic tune once more to take all the children away from the village, never to be seen again. The story was popularised in the nineteenth century by the Brothers Grimm and in a poem by Robert Browning. Just as the villagers had to pay the piper one way or the other, so, ultimately, must we.

Peter Out

Think of watching the last flames of a bonfire gradually die out on a cold November's evening, or of seeing a child's enthusiasm for his once-new toy fade on 26 December. Both are instances of something 'petering out', which means to come gradually to an end. The phrase first appeared in America in the mid-nineteenth century, though its origins are hazy. It is quite widely accepted that it originated in the mining industry of the time. Many people favour the idea that the word comes from 'saltpetre', which was one of the ingredients in the explosives used in mining. When a seam of gold was exhausted it was said to have 'petered out' because the explosives had allowed access to all the gold there was.

Nevertheless, alternative theories abound that have nothing to do with mining. One suggestion is that the expression has biblical origins and refers to the apostle Peter. The Gospel of John relates that, when Jesus was arrested, an impassioned Peter launched a staunch defence of Christ, but by the time the new day broke, his enthusiasm had dwindled, or 'petered out' as we might say, to the point that he denied even knowing Christ no fewer than three times.

Another idea is that the phrase derives from the French word *péter*. As well as meaning to fart, this means to fizzle or fizzle out, as in the phrase *péter dans la main*, or to fart in the hand – that is, to come to nothing.

Pieces of Eight

Any fans of old pirate yarns and movies will be familiar with the phrase 'pieces of eight'. Who could forget Long John Silver's parrot in *Treasure Island* squawking it repeatedly? But what did the infernal bird mean? Well, a piece of eight was a Spanish dollar, first minted and authorised for use in 1497. This went on to effectively become the first world currency, as it was used throughout Europe and both North and South America, and was still legal tender in the United States in the nineteenth century.

The 'eight' refers to the fact that, just as the pound is composed of 100 pence, the piece of eight equalled eight *reale*; sometimes it was even cut up to make this smaller-denomination coin. It was common practice at the time to refer to a coin as a 'piece of'. During the Golden Age of Piracy, between the 1650s and the 1720s, large quantities of the piece of eight were minted in the Americas and transported by sea back to Spain, making them attractive targets to pirates. Long John Silver's parrot was simply echoing the excitement generated by this money.

Pour Oil on Troubled Waters

To 'pour oil on troubled waters' is to address a conflict or volatile situation in such a manner as to placate the people concerned and bring calm. We've all attempted this with varying degrees of success, whether intervening in an argument between friends or colleagues or just trying to get kids to stop quarrelling. Since the sixteenth century 'troubled waters' have signified mental turmoil, and the fact that oil can calm actual stormy waters was known to the Ancient Greeks. However, its figurative use as we understand it today dates no further back than the end of the eighteenth century.

Put a Spoke in Your Wheel

When someone 'puts a spoke in your wheel' they are aiming to thwart your plans. But why would another spoke matter? Well, if the expression produces a mental image of a bicycle wheel, with its countless spokes, put it out of your mind. This expression goes back to the seventeenth century and refers to the carts of the time, which had solid wheels with a single hole in them. To insert a 'spoke', which here means simply a length of wood, into this hole would act as a brake, impeding the driver's progress.

Put the Screws on

To 'put the screws on' someone is to exert great pressure on them in order to achieve a specific outcome. For example, the leaders of powerful countries often put the screws, in the form of trade sanctions or the threat of invasion, on leaders of alleged 'rogue states' in an effort to make them abandon the development of nuclear weapons. These figurative 'screws' allude to the medieval torture device known as thumbscrews, which would be fastened to a victim's thumbs or fingers and tightened progressively until he yielded a confession or other desired information. Nowadays the screws may be metaphorical but they are still intended to cause pain.

Round Robin

A 'round robin' can be used to describe a petition to someone in which the order of signing of the signatories has been disguised (so as to protect the identity of the instigator). However, more recently the term has been used to mean a circular, such as a letter, flyer or email (think of the humorous emails in round-robin form) sent to a group of people. It is also used in sports: in a round-robin tournament each team or participant within a group plays all of the others an equal number of times (the group stages in football tournaments are a good example).

To get to the root of the phrase we need to go

back to the eighteenth century. British sailors of the time had to accept the complete command of their captain, or face the death penalty for mutiny. But a captain couldn't hang the whole disgruntled crew, and the sailors would petition their captain to vocalise their grievances by signing their names in a circle in order to conceal the ringleader's identity. The first use of this device is believed to have occurred in 1730. The rotational aspect of the communication – it passes around a group of people – seems to explain its use as a description of circular letters and emails, and indeed its use in sports.

Some sources claim that 'round robin' is a corruption of the French *ruban rond*, meaning round ribbon, and that the expression predates the British Navy and derives from similar petitions presented to the authorities in seventeenth-century France, but evidence for this is sketchy.

Run Amok

To 'run amok' means to shed your inhibitions and behave wildly and uncontrollably, as if in a frenzy. The expression originates from Malaysia, the Malaysian word *amuk* translating as 'uncontrollable rage'. In the early sixteenth century, Portuguese explorers in Malaysia wrote of indigenous people who would work themselves up into a state of mania before killing at random anyone who stood in their way. They referred to these people as *amuco*, and various explanations have been put forward as to their murderous behaviour. One idea was that drugs were responsible, another was that the killers simply 'snapped' after their fiercely hierarchical society was disrupted, and another still suggested that it was the expression of a strange code of honour between warriors.

What is clear is that 'amuk' entered English some time in the seventeenth century and was used to describe any kind of frenzied madman, not just a Malaysian. And, in the following century, Captain Cook made reference to running 'amok'. Today we use the expression to describe a state of febrile abandon, often accompanied by wanton destruction, but it no longer has any racial connotations.

Run into the Ground

If we 'run into the ground' a topic of conversation, an object or even a person, we overuse it or them so much that the result is destruction. You might say you've run yourself into the ground if you've had a particularly stressful and exhausting period in your life. The phrase probably derived from hunting, where a hunter might chase a fox until it is literally run into the ground – meaning its grave – and is believed to have come into use in the nineteenth century.

Scot-free

When someone goes, or gets off, 'scot-free', it means they have escaped any consequences or punishment for an action seen as calling for retribution. First, let's clear up the most common misconception: the expression has nothing to do with Scottish people and their alleged frugality with money. The 'scot' in question actually derives from the Old Norse word *skot*, meaning payment or contribution, which described a tax levied on the population from the thirteenth century onwards. To evade paying taxes was, in an expression that came into use in the sixteenth century, to go 'scot-free'. The word 'scot' also described money owed for drinks and entertainment, and those who escaped paying this likewise went scot-free.

Shilly-shally

If you 'shilly-shally', you are unable to make up your mind about something. The expression dates from the early eighteenth century and is a simple example of a phrase being made up in order to create a punchy, sonorous effect. In this case, 'shill' is a lesser form of 'shall' and the phrase is a 'varied reduplication' of 'Shall I?' Reduplication is a grammatical term for the repetition of a syllable, sometimes with a vowel change, as in this example or 'hurly-burly'.

Shoddy
The word 'shoddy' was borrowed from the wool trade to denote something of inferior quality. In the nineteenth century the term described inferior wool – the fluff collected during wool production – and itself derived from 'shoad', a seventeenth-century word used in mining to mean loose bits of ore. Both 'shoad' and 'shoddy' came from the Old English word 'scadan', meaning to separate or divide, the sense being that, in one case, fragments of ore, and in the other, second-rate wool, had become separated from a more valuable whole.

Sleep on a Clothes Line
When you're really exhausted you might say you could 'sleep on a clothes line'. It's hard to imagine this evocative phrase has any grounding in reality,

yet it does. In the late nineteenth and early twentieth centuries a number of lodging houses in Britain offered a '2d rope'. Men and women in extreme poverty would pay 2d (about 1p) to sit with others on a bench and lean on this rope or washing line strung across a room and fall asleep. If slumbers came, a rude awakening was in store at 5am, when an attendant would cut the rope.

Snog

Those from outside the British Isles might not be familiar with this word, though 'making out' for the Americans and 'pashing' for the Australians may ring a bell, as a snog is a nice, long, passionate kiss. Mmm, lovely. Many a young scamp has been caught snogging behind the school bike sheds, for it is a slang expression more readily associated with young people. Or at least the under-forties! As with much slang, the origins are hard to pin down precisely, though it certainly came into common use late in the twentieth century and is likely to have derived from 'snug', meaning very close.

Spendthrift

If spending means parting with money and thrift means frugality and economical providence, how did 'spendthrift' come to mean someone who spends money easily and wastefully? The key to the puzzle is the original sense of thrift. It meant savings, so a person who spends thrift is someone who spends these.

Stew in Your Own Juice

If you're allowed to 'stew in your own juice', you're left to suffer the consequences of your actions, the 'juice' being your anxious predicament. The expression came into use late in the nineteenth century, but it derives from one that is five centuries older, 'fry in your own grease'. To suffer this gruesome fate was to be burned at the stake.

Taxi

The first 'taxicabs' hit London's streets in 1903, and were so-called because each was fitted with a 'taximeter'. Invented in Germany by Wilhelm Bruhn in 1891, this device recorded distance and time in order to put an end to disputes over cab fares. The 'taxi' in 'taximeter' referred to the 'tax', or fare, that was being measured. It wasn't long before the taxicab was being referred to simply as a 'taxi'.

That's the Ticket!

Is there a reader of, say, fifty or above who can honestly say they've never announced, even in jest, 'That's the ticket!' when they've heard an answer or obtained something they really wanted? It's an affirmative expression intended to convey the message, 'That's just right, exactly what's needed.' The prosaic explanation of the origins of this phrase is that in the nineteenth century the poor were given tickets for soup kitchens, so 'That's the ticket for soup' came into use, and our phrase derived from this. However, the seemingly far-fetched yet more likely version is that it is actually an American slang mangling of the French word *étiquette* – which we're all familiar with as meaning right and proper behaviour. 'That's etiquette', the English version of the French expression *C'est l'étiquette*, was mispronounced to give 'That's the ticket'. There's a nice bit of symmetry in this derivation too, as the word *étiquette* derived from *estiquette*, which meant a ticket or label. Such tickets had instructions for proper behaviour written upon them.

Through Thick and Thin

To stay with someone or stick to some course of action 'through thick and thin' is to persevere with the situation through the bad times as well as the good, overcoming difficulties on the way. The phrase has been with us for a very long time: the earliest recorded use occurred in Chaucer's *Canterbury Tales* in the fourteenth century. At this time England was primarily woodland and there were few roads, so journeys could be long and arduous. Travelling 'through thicket and thin wood', the expression which gave us the modern idiom embraced both difficult and easy-going.

To the Manner (Manor) Born

'To the manor born,' you might say in mock-haughty fashion as you raise a glass to friends when indulging in something regarded as, well, a little posh. The phrase means to be accustomed to and well versed in the ways of the upper classes – or so you might think. It's true that 'to the manor born' is widespread and seems a reasonable thing to say in jest, but in fact it derives from a far older expression where 'manor' was 'manner' and it has nothing to do with the aristocracy. Centuries ago it was used to describe someone who, by birth, is predisposed to the customs and practices of the people and is able to behave accordingly. Shakespeare had Hamlet say it best: 'And to the manner born, it is a custom, more honoured in the breach than the observance.'

So just how did 'manor' creep in? Well, while the expression based on 'manner' came to us by courtesy of Shakespeare in the early seventeenth century, the more popular saying is of 1970s vintage, and replaced the earlier version in everyday speech. For this you can blame Peter Spence, the creator of the BBC's sitcom *To The Manor Born*, which first aired in 1979. His title with its pun on Shakespeare's words, and the show's ensuing massive popularity, spread the idea that this was the original expression. The Bard must be turning in his grave.

Upset the Apple Cart

We'd all do best not to 'upset the apple cart' if we want to avoid messing up the status quo, causing trouble and upset, and spoiling the best-laid plans and all that. The expression has its origins in Roman times, when people would say, *'Plaustrum perculi'*, or 'I've upset the cart', which has the same figurative meaning as the phrase we use today. But it wasn't until the eighteenth century that the cart became specifically an apple cart. It's a wonderful image: the farmer's cart upset, apples flying this way and that, chaos ensuing. Sometimes the expression is used slightly differently – to 'upset *someone's* apple cart' – but it means the same.

Wet Blanket

Those of us who know someone whose very presence puts a stop to fun and high jinks are unfortunate enough to be acquainted with a 'wet blanket'. The metaphor is clear enough – that of a wet blanket smothering a flame – and it is related to a similar saying, 'to put a dampener' on something, which means to take the joy from it. But what about the expression's origin? Well, some would have you believe it's 1920s American slang, but in fact it can be traced back to nineteenth-century Scotland, where it occurred in Scottish writer John Galt's 1830 novel *Lawrie Todd*.

With Bells on

'I'll be there with bells on!' you might respond to an invitation that sounds irresistible. The phrase dates back to the end of the nineteenth century or the early twentieth and bears an uncanny resemblance to the expression 'with knobs on'. Many a commentator has a favourite theory as to the origin of the bells, but it seems likely that it is from the practice of decorating a horse-drawn carriage with bells and suchlike for special occasions.

As for the knobs, they refer to the brass knobs on the bedposts of well-to-do members of society. The expression was used as a rejoinder to a challenge or comment, and the important thing was that it conveyed a bit of one-upmanship: 'Whatever you might do to me, the same back to you – with knobs on.'

Without Rhyme or Reason

When we say that something has occurred 'without rhyme or reason', we mean that we're absolutely stumped, baffled, clueless – we just cannot figure out a clear explanation for it. The expression comes from French, and the earlier form *'ne ryme, ne reason'* appeared in an English translation of a French farce. The poet John Skelton picked it up – 'For reason can I none find, Nor good rhyme in your matter' – though we can thank good old Shakespeare for popularising it. He was rather fond of the expression, using it throughout his work.

INDEX